Praise for Dorr
There's a St

"I recommend this book to every church leader that believes 'the church has the potential to be an instrument of healing in a world that is full of pain.' Yet, the church's healing virtue will not be realized through belief alone but also through theologically informed and practically equipped leaders properly responding to polarizing racial division and tragedies in their churches and communities. Located at the intersection of Public Administration and the Judeo-Christian prophetic tradition, Dorrell's 'Racial Crisis Framework: realization, readiness, responsiveness, and renewal' is a fresh, provocative perspective. Rife with practical insight and theological depth, this book is a must read for all who desire to lead faithfully and responsibly during turbulent times."

—Rev. Dr. Bankole Akinbinu, Pastor at Baptist Grove Church (Raleigh, NC)

"Dr. Harold Dorrell Briscoe is proving to be a beacon of hope and insightful stewardship as he stimulate the urgency of the church to recall its purpose in standing for what's right of its people. While social issues continue to diversify their display, the underlying root causes still exist. Dr. Briscoe portrays and pronounces the very actions needed to realign God's people with purpose and pompous."

—Leonardo Williams, Community Activist, Serial Entrepreneur, Educator

"If there has ever been a moment in history that begs for a book like this, it's now. Drawing on his backgrounds in disaster resiliency and Christian theology, Dr. Harold Dorrell Briscoe offers a desperately needed guide for church leaders looking to navigate the destructive racial storms of 21st century America. Much like the climate crisis,

Briscoe shows that the current atmosphere of racial tension requires thoughtful and courageous mitigation efforts from those who lead America's churches. But 'without knowledge, the people perish,' and, far too often, white pastors and leaders lack the historical-contextual understanding of the black experience needed to lead their congregations and communities through these racial storms. But Briscoe offers both buoyant hope and concrete help to move us forward together toward a future that restores and rebuilds after the storm."

—Tim Staier, Lead Pastor, Elevate Life Church (Jacksonville, FL)

"Dr. Briscoe gives us an impassioned, fervent, uniquely Christian tract for the times. Now, more than ever, we need his word of truth. North American Christians live in a storm of racialized fury that is a test of our Christian faith. Briscoe not only truthfully names that storm but also shows us how churches and believers can not only survive its ravages but also thrive as those whom Christ is busy delivering from the sin of racism. To my fellow church leaders I say, 'Desperate for a way through America's racial past and present? Read this book.'"

—Will Willimon, Professor of the Practice of Christian Ministry, Duke University, author of *Who Lynched Willie Earle?: Preaching to Confront Racism.*

"I know many people of many colors who would love to see the ugly specter of racism disappear, but who simply do not know how to fight the cultural systems and norms that sustain and support it. Dr. Briscoe lays out a clear four-step program to help leaders through the hard work of walking with a group or congregation to build awareness and the willingness to actively respond that will lead to a better world."

—Rev. Dr. Larry Duggins, Executive Director & Leader Missional Wisdom Foundation

"Honest. Pastoral. Prophetic. Dr. Dorrell Briscoe delivers a timely prophetic word to the church. He invites the church to come and learn about racism and holds up a mirror to expose the places it has seeped into the pews. His work comparing the lack of preparation when Hurricane Katrina hit New Orleans to the lack of preparation in the church when racialized storms hit is a poignant call to the church to do the work to shore up its levies against racism. The church needs Dorrell's voice now more than ever!"

—REV. DR. JENN GRAFFIUS, DIRECTOR OF MENTORING AND FORMATION, AZUSA PACIFIC UNIVERSITY

"Dorrell brings together the best of his knowledge of scripture and theology with models from the secular world for the purpose of offering to pastors, lay people, and congregations a way to respond that is rooted in the love of God and love of neighbor. I commend to you this book, the witness therein, and the wisdom offered for the blessing of your ministry."

—THE REV. DR. TIMOTHY MENTZER, SENIOR PASTOR, HOLY TRINITY LUTHERAN CHURCH (LANCASTER, PA)

"*There's a Storm Comin'* is a must read for church leaders who are interested in finding solutions to America's problem of race. In drawing from various disciplines, this thought-provoking work uses mitigation strategies that allow congregational leaders to engage in best practices that minimize damage from America's racialized storms, through the lens of prophetic leadership. I intend to use its strategies in my ministry and I highly encourage others to do the same."

—JONATHAN C. AUGUSTINE, SENIOR PASTOR, ST. JOSEPH AME CHURCH (DURHAM, NC); NATIONAL CHAPLAIN, ALPHA PHI ALPHA FRATERNITY, INC.

There's a Storm Comin'

There's a Storm Comin'

*How the American Church Can Lead
Through Times of Racial Crisis*

Dr. Harold Dorrell Briscoe Jr.

ISBN: 9798649561785
Imprint: Independently published

FIRST EDITION

Cover and graphic design by Elizabeth Curl

www.dorrellbriscoe.com

*To my kings: George Floyd, Ahmaud Arbery,
Philando Castile, and Alton Sterling*

*To my queens: Atatiana Jefferson, Breonna Taylor,
and Sandra Bland*

*May your legacies continue to whisper to us and
may you all rest in power.*

Contents

Foreword   ix

Introduction   xi

Part One: Realization   20
I: [Sociopolitical] Climate Change   23
II: What Are Racialized Crises?   44
III: The Ineffectiveness of the Church   51

Part Two: Readiness   76
IV: The Need for Awareness   79
V: Establishing Readiness Through   87
Climate Change Adaptation and Natural
Disaster Mitigation Strategies

Part Three: Responsiveness   106
VI: Insights from the Prophetic Tradition   109
VII: Responding in the Midst of the Storm: 129
Two Sermons and a Blog on Racial Reconciliation

Part Four: Renewal   154
VIII: Racialized Crises as Catalytic Events   157

Conclusion   168

Acknowledgments   172

About the Author   176

Notes   177

Foreword

I don't believe in coincidence. As I pulled up a chair to my desk to write this Foreword, my heart is aching after hearing the news of the death of a black man in Minneapolis at the hands of police officers. My heart ache is a reaction of being human, but it is also the ache of a father who has a black son. I have not shied away from preaching the Word of God as it convicts each of us and as it gives us a vision of God's eternal way of living. The members of the white congregation of which I am one of the pastors hears me. They are moved by my tears and heartache. And, they say, "The pastor is biased because he has a black son."

As I have struggled with racism in light of the Word of God, I have searched for guidance in my preaching, teaching, leading, and community engagement. Dorrell Briscoe has become one of the lighthouses to which I turn. I met Dorrell on the first day of our doctoral program at Duke University Divinity School. This fast friendship has been one of the best blessings in my life. He has quickly become a mentor to my son, and I am so deeply blessed to have his children call me Uncle Tim. His love for the Lord and for all that the Lord loves is extraordinary. He has a remarkable capacity to analyze a problem, clearly express the situation, and provide wisdom and guidance.

Dorrell believes that the church is called to "respond to …racially charged tragedies in a way that brings healing and hope to individuals, communities, and cities plagued with despair." The church will be at its best in that response if the church is prepared.

Having been a parish pastor for twenty-five years, I have

lost count of how many times, after a tragedy has struck our parish or community, people will say, "What can we do?" In the elevated fear, anxiety, and anger, our capacity to imagine solutions is remarkably limited. We do our "just above mediocrity" best, until the next time. This approach is reactive and thus, limited.

What would happen, however, if we were prepared? Is it possible to move from reaction to response? Perhaps we can find ways to make difficult situations better instead of worse. Could we defuse a volatile situation? Dorrell believes the answer is yes. The severity of a crisis, he believes, can be mitigated.

Dorrell brings together the best of his knowledge of scripture and theology with models from the secular world for the purpose of offering to pastors, lay people, and congregations a way to respond that is rooted in the love of God and love of neighbor.

I commend to you this book, the witness therein, and the wisdom offered for the blessing of your ministry.

—*The Rev. Dr. Timothy Mentzer*
Senior Pastor, Holy Trinity Lutheran Church
Lancaster, Pennsylvania

Introduction

The first week of July 2016 was tumultuous. The nation was rocked by two killings of black men at the hands of law enforcement officials. On July 5, 2016, Alton Sterling died in Baton Rouge, Louisiana, after an altercation with police officers. Philando Castile was shot and killed the next day after alerting a police officer that he was legally carrying a gun. On July 7, 2016, five Dallas police officers were gunned down at a peaceful protest in downtown Dallas.

The fires of anger and fear burned through social media sites all over the country and in my own congregation. The string of deaths made national and international headlines. Former presidents Barack Obama and George W. Bush spoke at the Dallas Memorial Service for the five police officers. Both attempted to heal the gaping racial wound— reopened by these events—by reminding Americans of our shared commitment to the nation's intrinsic values of compassion, empathy, and unity.

The string of racially charged tragedies was causing enormous psychological and social disruption throughout the nation. This was a racialized crisis.[i] I was struck by the silence of white pastors and the racial strife that occurred in my church. I realized that if the church is to respond to these racially charged tragedies in a way that brings healing and hope to individuals, communities, and cities plagued with despair, it must prepare for them. The church is meant to proclaim salvation, reconciliation, and equality. Scripture is full of stories and passages that communicate God's heart for justice. Historically, the church (or at least some churches) has boldly taken a stand against slavery, lynching, Jim Crow, and other events, systems, and people that have undercut civil rights. Scripture communicates God's heart for the vulnerable, and people are looking for how the church will respond to these racialized calamities.

Police shootings of unarmed black people and other racially charged issues are intense for individuals and communities. This project will not discuss the debate surrounding their causes or whether such shootings were justified. I aim to discuss the unrest they generate and recommend strategies to mitigate that unrest before the racialized crises occurs. Additionally, I intend to lay out a plan that effectively responds to the racialized storms and the unrest they generate in a community and congregational context.

This book will explore strategies and research from the fields of climate change adaptation and natural disaster mitigation and adapt them to a church context to create a practical framework that helps faith leaders prepare for and respond to racialized crises in their communities and congregations. The aim in this project is to research and recommend best practices from these scientific disciplines and synthesize these strategies with a prophetic and theological response that give churches a roadmap for reducing the psychological distress in their communities and among their congregants. My hope is that the information in this book could be applied to a variety of sectors across our society.

American Christian leaders have a limited toolkit and framework to deal with racialized crises and I believe that methods from the field of disaster resilience can be used to assist faith leaders. Similar to Brenda Salter McNeil's statement of intent in her groundbreaking *Roadmap to Reconciliation*, my own expectation "is that this model will illuminate and energize our imagination for what is possible, so together we can create a new reality of reconciliation in communities around the world."[ii]

In this book, I make the case that faith leaders should think and act from a perspective of mitigation concerning racialized crises. Racialized crises are traumatic events that make national headlines and disrupt the sociopolitical landscape of our country, cities, and communities. These crises affect institutions and produce a high degree of psychological distress in individuals.

The term "crisis" refers essentially to an unexpected circumstance. "A crisis marks a phase of disorder in the development of a person, an organization, a community, an ecosystem, a business sector, or a polity." While not every crisis can be foreseen, we can learn from the past to become more resilient and responsive in the future.

Mitigation is all about taking proactive measures to reduce the severity and impact of an event. Mitigation is an important public policy strategy that is used in local, state, and federal governments. The Federal Emergency Management Agency defines mitigation as "actions that involve lasting, often permanent, reduction of, exposure to, probability of, or potential loss from hazard events."[iii]

How should the church respond to these tragedies? What strategies should be implemented to prepare for these tumultuous times? How can the church reduce the psychological distress of its congregants? What steps should the church take to close the racial gaps that widen when sociopolitical unrest is generated? What Biblical themes should the church prioritize and communicate during these times?

I intend to offer a simultaneous sociopolitical and prophetic response to these racialized crises to offer faith and organizational leaders a framework for preparing their churches and organizations when these events occur. By integrating my prior experiences as a pastor, public policy official, and my research in the field of disaster resilience and urban planning I developed a framework that hopefully equips faith leaders with proper insights and strategies to lead their churches during times of sociopolitical unrest from racialized

The Racial Crisis Framework consists of four parts. The first, Realization, involves an analysis of what has and is changing America's sociopolitical climate and why that change is exacerbating racial tension. This section defines the concept of racialized crises and will reveal why they hurt the church. To effectively mitigate the severity of crises, we must understand what they are and what key elements give them intensity.

Part two, Readiness, analyzes the terms adaptation, mitigation, and preparedness. These concepts, if employed by church leadership, can enable churches and organizations to be better prepared in the face of worsening race relations. I propose different ways faith leaders can build readiness in their churches and organizations.

Part three, Responsiveness, highlights how to respond to racialized tragedies. This section involves an analysis of prophetic imagination and leadership as a model that can aid pastors in addressing racialized storms. Sermons will be presented as an example of mitigating racial tension during times of unrest.

Part four is entitled Renewal. This part focuses on what we can learn from these predicaments and how we can change as a result of what we learn. Chapter ten explains how racialized catastrophes can be catalytic events that spark needed change in a congregation.

I believe there are religious leaders that desire to speak out and lead their churches in the mission of racial healing, but they don't know where to start. The enormity and complexity of this issue can be daunting. However, it would be wise to remember Jesus's words to the disciples in the book of Matthew: "Jesus looked at them and said, 'With man this is impossible, but with God all things are possible.'"[iv] It is possible to bridge the racial divide in America.

While this book will focus a great deal on the intersection of race relations in America and the church, I do not intend to offer here a model for racial reconciliation or a strategy for solving structural and interpersonal racism. There are solid and informative books on those topics. The focus here is narrower: it seeks to lay out a strategy to enable faith leaders to reduce the severity and disruption of highly publicized and polarized racial tragedies within their churches and communities.

The church can take the lead in communicating hope to the world in the midst of despair. The church has the potential to be an instrument of healing in a world that is full of pain. This book, I hope, will help churches be that instrument and play the sweet music of reconciliation and healing that our country so desperately needs to hear.

There's a Storm Comin':

*How the American Church Can Lead
Through Times of Racial Crisis*

Institutional Mitigation of Racialized Tragedies

REALIZATION

RACIAL CRISIS
FRAMEWORK

RENEWAL

READINESS

RESPONSIVENESS

PART ONE

REALIZATION

Institutional Mitigation of Racialized Tragedies

This section focuses on key events and figures that have drastically altered the calculus of America's sociopolitical climate, breaks down the concept of racialized storms, and elaborates on why these storms are detrimental to the church. The fundamental point in this section is to generate awareness of what a racialized crisis is and why they hurt congregations.

Awareness is critical to action. Christian leaders must understand the elements that make up these tragedies and why it is so detrimental to their congregants, especially people of color who attend their church. Realization is the key to unlocking action. This is a journey, an educative process, that exposes church leaders to the painful issues that comprise our present-day racial inequalities.

It is imperative that contemporary Christian leaders ascertain the extent of America's history of racial injustices, present-day structural inequalities, and racial disparities. This learning process is critical to leading effectively during racialized crises in America. Many white Christian pastors simply do not know what to say during these times because they have not committed to learn about the cultural issues that black and brown people deal with. They have no context to draw from, no knowledge to utilize, and thus remain silent during times of racial unrest.

Leading through these predicaments starts with realizing that there is a storm coming and taking the necessary precautions to prepare your staff and churches is imperative. Times are changing and America's race relations are growing worse. It is time for the American church to divert its attention and resources to bridging the racial divide, quelling tension, and being a beacon of healing and hope for the surrounding communities and cities they reside in.

I

[Sociopolitical] Climate Change

America is in trouble — perhaps most of it — has to do with race. Everywhere we turn, there is discord and division, death and destruction. When we survey the land, we see a country full of suffering that cannot fully understand, and a history that we can no longer deny.

—MICHAEL ERIC DYSON, *TEARS WE CANNOT STOP*

Global Climate Change

On December 12, 2015, nearly two hundred nations, led by the United States, came together in Paris to seriously address global climate change by signing the Paris Climate Accord, otherwise known as The Paris Agreement. This agreement's "central aim is to strengthen the global response to the threat of climate change by keeping a global temperature rise this century well below 2 degrees Celsius above pre-industrial levels and to pursue efforts to limit the temperature increase even further to 1.5 degrees Celsius."[v] The Paris Agreement "requires countries to set their own targets for reducing emissions by 2020. The Obama administration committed the U.S. to reducing carbon emissions by 26 to 28% by 2025.[vi] This was an extraordinary moment in world history as nearly every nation on earth came together to mitigate the threat of global climate change.

When the sun shines, it warms the Earth, but an accumulation of greenhouse gases like CO_2 and methane prevent the sun's radiation from bouncing back into space. These gases essentially trap heat. According to the Intergovernmental Panel on Climate Change, "Scientific evidence for warming of the climate system is unequivocal."[vii] Remarkably, there is near-universal consensus among climatologists and climate scientists that the Earth's global climate is changing. "Ninety-seven percent of climate scientists agree that climate-warming trends over the past century are very likely due to human activities, and most of the leading scientific organizations worldwide have issued public statements endorsing this position."[viii]

Rapid climate change has compelled industry leaders and government officials to introduce sweeping changes as to how they do business in hopes of mitigating the harmful effects of global climate change. Warming oceans, shrinking ice sheets, glacial retreat, decreased snow cover, sea level rise, declining Arctic sea ice, ocean acidification, extreme weather events, and global temperature rise are all the result of rapid global climate change.[ix]

Whether it's a severe drought in California, soaring temperatures in Arizona, massive amounts of precipitation in the Midwest, or powerful hurricanes that strike the Gulf coast, more and more people are becoming aware of the seriousness of climate change and the potential ramifications it brings to our country's ecological and economic footprint.

I had the privilege of studying public administration with an emphasis on urban revitalization and disaster resilience in graduate school at Texas A&M University. My final project, *Adaptation to Climate Change in the Houston-Galveston Area: Perceptions and Prospects*, was inspired by Hurricane Katrina's devastation and the growing consensus in the scientific community that climate change is an enormous threat that is leaving coastal communities increasingly vulnerable. The project focused on climate change adaptation and mitigation strategies in the Houston-Galveston region. I researched and recommended policy initiatives and funding options that could enhance the interoperability of communication between local, state, and federal officials. My research focused on fostering greater collaboration of institutional structures and recommended greater legislative authority to implement transportation infrastructure investments that could build greater resilience in municipalities across the Houston-Galveston region.

The project's aim was to give municipalities a plan that would help reduce the vulnerability their communities faced as the risk of powerful hurricanes striking the region increased. Innovative and effective mitigation *before* the storm was imperative so officials could focus on public safety, coordination, and execution, instead of being hamstrung due to faulty equipment and poor communication.[x] As I worked with city officials and industry leaders, I saw firsthand how the "ah-ha moment" occurs: a moment of realization, when they started to realize that they were vulnerable to the consequences of climate change.

> It was not the purpose of this study to determine the cause of climate change, but to look at the evidence provided by scientific organizations and determine how the effects of climate change should alter the decision-making process among officials with authority over public infrastructure.[xi]

While the Earth's climate has undergone profound changes within the last fifty years due to human-made carbon emissions—now leaving millions who live in coastal communities vulnerable—the sociopolitical climate in America has drastically changed during the last twelve years and is (with a constellation of other disparities) producing social vulnerability in individuals, communities, neighborhoods, and cities across the nation.

Similar to the greenhouses gases (such as carbon dioxide and methane that human activity creates) that have contributed to a rise in global temperatures, there have been a number of sociopolitical events that have changed America.

This sociopolitical climate change is largely responsible for the racial unrest and tension that Americans experience today. The parallels between actual global climate change and sociopolitical climate change are strikingly similar. Both consist of man-made elements that contribute to their exacerbation. Both, if left unchecked, can have enormous consequences on their respective landscapes. Both, if taken seriously, can be mitigated through a series of proactive measures and strategies that can potentially reduce their severity among individuals and communities.

Before examining racialized crises—what they are, how they affect the church, and how to prepare and respond to them—I intend to briefly describe eight factors that have changed America's sociopolitical climate. I believe that these eight factors are converging and are largely responsible for U.S. race relations being at their lowest point in decades.

The eight factors are: the election of Barack Obama, the rise of the Alt-Right, Census Bureau projections that predict changing racial demographics in America, the rise of the Black Lives Matter movement, technological advances in social media platforms, Ferguson and the highly publicized police shootings of unarmed black men, and the election of Donald Trump have all had and continue to make a drastic impact on the social fabric of America.

The Election of Barack Obama

Nearly fifty years ago, Bobby Kennedy eerily predicted the ascendancy of a black man to the U.S. presidency. "Things are moving so fast in race relations. A Negro could be president in forty years. There is no question about it. In the next forty years, a Negro can achieve that same position that my brother [John F. Kennedy] has."[xii] Kennedy predicted that ascendancy to the exact year. Forty years later, Barack Obama, a charismatic senator from Illinois, was voted in as the 44th president of the United States.

The election of Barack Obama was an earthquake in the history of American politics. As the first person of color to win the presidency, the historic moment could not be understated. Tim Wise said it well, "For a nation built on a foundation of slavery, disenfranchisement, and white domination, the election of a man of color...to the highest office in the land, is of no small import."[xiii] President Obama's ascendancy to the White House was a major change to America's sociopolitical climate. Numerous political pundits and newspapers joyfully applauded Obama's election as a clear sign that the United States was finally moving to a post-racial society where racial differences would be a thought of the past—a society where an ideology of colorblindness would be the default lens of how Americans deal with racial progress.

The optimism was short-lived. Early into his first term, President Obama made national news early during the arrest of renowned Harvard Scholar, Henry Louis Gates Jr. Asked to comment on the affair, Obama claimed, "that the Cambridge police acted stupidly in arresting somebody when there was already proof that they were in their own home."[xiv] That hit a nerve. President Obama touched on the highly charged political issue of police brutality on African Americans. The backlash was swift and it was reported that the president was shocked by the subsequent fallout he received from his comments. Barack Obama campaigned on change and hope, but his eight years in office was mired by racially tinged rhetoric, an unprecedented level of obstructionism, and hyper-partisanship from Republicans. Indeed, Peniel Joseph writes:

> Almost immediately, the Obama presidency unleashed racial furies that have only multiplied over time. From the tea party's racially tinged attacks on the president's policy agenda to the birther movement's more overtly racist fantasies asserting that Obama was not even an American citizen, the national racial climate grew more, and not less, fraught. If racial conflict, in the form of birthers, tea partyers, and gnawing resentments, implicitly shadowed Obama's first term, it erupted into open warfare during much of his second.[xv]

Furthermore, a string of high-profile deaths of black men at the hands of police officers consistently aggravated the deep racial wound in America. If the president spoke on any of these situations his comments were met with a swift and strong backlash from white conservatives, angry that Obama mentioned race at all. For instance, after seventeen-year-old Trayvon Martin lost his life at the hands of George Zimmerman in an Orlando suburb, a colossal amount social unrest and nation-wide protests were generated. President Obama, in an unscheduled visit to the White House Press Room, commented on the situation.

> You know, when Trayvon Martin was first shot I said that this could have been my son. Another way of saying that is Trayvon Martin could have been me thirty-five years ago. And when you think about why, in the African American community at least, there's a lot of pain around what happened here, I think it's important

to recognize that the African American community is looking at this issue through a set of experiences and a history that doesn't go away.[xvi]

Conservative analysts were highly critical of the president's comments. However, some conservative commentators criticized Obama for what they called divisiveness by speaking as an African American instead of representing the entire country. Todd Starnes, a Fox News Radio anchor, tweeted "race-baiter in chief."[xvii] The Obama candidacy and presidency was a profound phenomenon in this history of America's sociopolitical landscape.

Census Bureau Projections

America's demographics are rapidly changing from fifty years ago when Caucasians made up nearly 80% of the population. "New population projections released this week by the Census Bureau indicate that the U.S. population will become 'majority minority' in 2044. At that time, whites will make up 49.7% of the population compared with 25% for Hispanics, 12.7% for blacks, 7.9% for Asians, and 3.7% for multiracial persons."[xviii]

When the Census Bureau came out with these projections, it generated a considerable amount of news. Impending shifts in America's racial composition has contributed to white anxiety and fear. Dr. Jennifer Richeson has recently coauthored two studies on "the effect of changing racial demographic shifts on racial attitudes and political ideology."[xix] Her research shows that as whites become aware of their potential minority status in the future there is an "increased erosion of progressive race-related social policy."[xx]

> A control group was given information on current U.S. demographics, while a test group was given census headlines using "majority-minority" language about the impending shift in racial demographics. White Americans who read about the demographic shift in California to a majority-minority state, for example, became more likely to endorse conservative race-related policies than those who did not—including among those who identify as moderate or progressive. Richeson suggested this evidence of shifting political allegiances is a function of "social identity threat"—the idea, she said, that "if racial minorities increase in status, they are likely to reduce the influence of white Americans in society...Kwon and Richeson agree that the findings suggest not just anxiety about minority groups increasing in size, but a fear that that may also mean corresponding loss of power.[xxi]

The concern of impending shifts in American racial demographics and the subsequent resentment and fear that has been produced is one of the reasons behind the rise of the ideology of white nationalism. Amanda Taub writes,

> For a long time, he said, white nationalism was less an ideology than the default presumption of American life. Until quite recently, white Americans could easily see the nation as essentially an extension of their own ethnic group. But the country's changing demographics, the civil rights movement and a push for multiculturalism in many quarters mean that white Americans are now confronting the prospect of a nation that is no longer built solely around their own identity.

> For many white people, of course, the growing diversity is something to celebrate. But for others it is a source of stress. The white nationalist movement has drawn support from that latter group. Its supporters argue that the United States should protect its white majority by sharply limiting immigration, and perhaps even by compelling nonwhite citizens to leave.[xxii]

As the reality of America becoming browner permeates the sociopolitical landscape, fear, resentment, and anxiety has pervaded many white people. An ABC News/*Washington Post* poll conducted during the 2016 presidential campaign revealed that "37% of his [Trump] supporters strongly believed that whites are losing out because of preferences for blacks and Hispanics."[xxiii] The issue of white anxiety over changing racial demographics is a significant development in America's sociopolitical climate.

Police Shootings of Unarmed Black Men

The highly publicized killings of unarmed African Americans have exacerbated racial tension in American society. Michael Brown was shot and killed in an altercation with Darren Wilson, a Ferguson police officer, on August 9, 2014. His dead body remained on the street for nearly four hours. He received no medical attention and was eventually taken away in a police van. Dozens of neighborhood residents watched in horror as his body lay in the hot August sun for hours. The underlying tension between the African American community and police had reached a boiling point has hundreds of residents burned with rage at the killing of Mike Brown. A deep communal mourning took place because many residents of Ferguson were intimately familiar with confrontation and unfair treatment by the Ferguson Police Department.

The ensuing days and weeks were marked with violent "protest and acts of vandalism in Ferguson, as well as widespread calls for an investigation into the incident. After a day of vigils, the looting of businesses, vandalizing vehicles, as well as protestor's clash with policemen occurred."xxiv The nation was blindsided by division, frustration, tension, turmoil, and hate. The tectonic plates of the American criminal justice system and racial inequalities collided and produced a race quake that shook America to its core. The unrest wasn't limited to a specific geographic locale. Protests occurred in hundreds of America cities. Marc Lamont Hill writes in *Nobody: Casualties of America's War on the Vulnerable, from Ferguson to Flint and Beyond:*

> In response to the grand jury's decision not to indict Darren Wilson, crowds of protesters appeared in Oakland, Los Angeles, Dallas, Denver, Washington, Minneapolis, Chicago, Atlanta, and New York to stand in solidarity. They wanted to see justice prevail in the particular instance.xxv

The civil unrest that was produced in Ferguson swept through American cities from Hoboken to Spokane; massive protest erupted from coast to coast as young people stood, marched, and disrupted the normal civil rhythms. The psychological trauma that Ferguson produced had a severe impact on the sociopolitical landscape in America. Nekima Levy-Armstrong writes in *Seeking Justice in the Age of Unrest*, "not since the Civil Rights Movement of the 1950s and 60s had we witnessed sustained waves of protests, demonstrations, and outcries against racial injustice in the

U.S., young folks in Ferguson marched to the frontlines of the battle for racial equality and forced America to hear their voices demanding justice."[xxvi] The death of Michael Brown and the subsequent verdict ruling officer Darren Wilson not guilty cut deeply into the heart of the African American community. Other high-profile killings including, Eric Garner, Freddie Gray, Philando Castile, Keith Lamont Scott, and Alton Sterling produced similar mass protest and social unrest.

The Rise of the Alt-Right

The Alt-Right has its origins in an online publication that Richard Spencer (a prominent white nationalist) debuted in 2010.[xxvii] The ideology essentially rejects mainstream conservativism because of a perceived focus on Jews and non-whites by traditional conservatives. This ideology focuses on a "race-infused brand of extreme conservatism" that advocates for white people as a group.[xxviii] "There are people with other beliefs who fall under the umbrella of the Alt-Right but all share a fixation on white identity as central to their ideology."[xxix] The movement has gained steam in recent years with Donald Trump's candidacy and presidency. "In recent months, a number of these Alt-Righters have promoted Donald Trump's presidential bid, seeing the populist candidate as someone tougher than so called 'cuckservatives,' thanks to his controversial stands on issues ranging from immigration to Muslims in America."[xxx]

The Alt-Right has grown in its popularity and influence in recent years. "Their goal is to influence mainstream whites by exposing them to the concept of white identity and racial consciousness."xxxi This is a movement that is profoundly influencing the sociopolitical climate in America. Looking across the sociopolitical landscape in America, one cannot deny the impact that the Alt-Right is having on conservatism and the discourse of race and identity in America.

Black Lives Matter

Black Lives Matter (BLM) was first used as a Twitter hashtag following the death of Trayvon Martin in 2012. BLM has been central in the conversation about police brutality in our mainstream political discourse.

> Born as a Twitter hashtag, Black Lives Matter has evolved into a potent alternative to the political paralysis and isolation that racial justice proponents have faced since the election of Obama. In just over two years, the young movement has reinvigorated confrontation politics, giving voice to a popular and righteous rage, establishing a new touchstone of grassroots resistance, and ending the acquiescence that has crippled progressive forces in the age of Obama. The upsurge, which has centered on the crucial, galvanizing issue of police misconduct, also shows signs of addressing larger questions of social inequity.xxxii

BLM is a social justice movement that is capturing the hearts of minds of young people of all colors.

> The organized demonstrations, protests and outrage of a new generation of civil rights activist turned the hashtag #blacklivesmatter into the clarion call for a new

Obama administration has not healed the America's centuries-old racial wound and it would be unwise to think that President Trump will successfully be able to quell the racial anxiety that exist in America.

Digital Interconnection

It is important to recognize how vulnerable churches are in the twenty-first century era of globalization and digital interconnection. Robert Miller writes in *Hurricane Katrina: Communication & Infrastructure Impacts*:

> As the twenty-first century goes along we will find ourselves paying more attention to the implications of vulnerabilities in our critical infrastructures. There's a reason for this concern, given the ways in which today's globalized, just in time, interconnected world magnifies the consequences of regional catastrophes. Globalization and interconnections mean that event which once could have been handled locally will have widespread ripple effects, and that these facts can be unexpectedly disruptive.[xxxv]

These racialized crises don't merely affect a specific locale—with the advent of social media and other technological and digital advances, the impact of these storms are felt all over the country. Eric Garner's death didn't just affect Staten Island; the shock and dismay was experienced across the country in Spokane. Walter Scott's death didn't merely affect North Charleston, but the pain could be felt as far as North Fort Myers, Florida.

Although Philando Castile was killed in Minnesota, the psychological storm surge disturbed the entire nation.

Because of Facebook's feature "Facebook live," millions of Americans were seeing live footage of a man dying in front of his girlfriend and her four-year-old daughter. The technological advances of the mobile/camera phone and the advent of social media have enabled emotional shockwaves to be felt beyond the epicenter where the tragedies occur.

Racialized crises hurt the church because of the magnitude of digital interconnection and the changing public sphere. "Americans are increasingly turning to social media for news and political information."[xxxvi] Facebook, Twitter, Instagram, YouTube, and other platforms have drastically changed the public sphere and are making civil discourse difficult to achieve. Monica Anderson and Paul Hitlin write in a Pew Research Center article, "Social Media Conversations about Race," that "these platforms have provided new arenas for national conversations about race and racial inequality."[xxxvii] Hitlin and Anderson describe how Twitter is now a platform that hosts discussions on race immediately after major news events.[xxxviii]

Technological advances in media have put a greater spotlight on the issue of police brutality. The beating of Rodney King is a clear example.

> The video footage vividly told the story of police brutality on television to a much wider audience. The police officers, who were acquitted of the crime, had hit King more than fifty times with their batons. Today, live streaming, tweets, and Facebook posts have blasted the incidents of police brutality, beyond the black community and into the mainstream media. Philando Castile's fiancée, Diamond Reynolds, who was in the car with her daughter when he was shot, streamed the immediate aftermath of the shooting on her phone using

Facebook live. "Modern technology allows, indeed insists, that the white community take notice of these kinds of situations and incidents."xxxix

The digital interconnection that exists today drives news cycles. The "trending" phenomenon brings events and ideas to the forefront of people's computers and phone screens.

Twitter is a platform that makes civil dialogue especially challenging, especially as Twitter posts are restricted to only 280 characters. Nikita Carney analyzes this phenomenon, noting:

> To effectively convey messages in so little space, words must be chosen carefully. To transpose Barthes's explanation about myth, each tweet must be crafted in a way to capture one's attention. Since the Twitter platform does not allow space for a lengthy, nuanced conversation to unfold, the importance of making an immediate impression is a central character of these debates on social media. The practice of "trolling," leaving incendiary comments with the intention of causing offense and eliciting a response, further amplifies the polarity of political conversations that unfold.xl

When the social unrest of Ferguson occurred, the images of violence and confrontation were quickly circulated in national and international news.xli Hundreds of journalists, from all over the United States and the world, traveled to Ferguson get a clear sense of what was happening on the ground. Social media exploded with "over 3.6 million posts appeared on Twitter documenting and reflecting on the emerging details surrounding Michael Brown's death."xlii A significant portion of the U.S. population now has video-enabled smartphones that allow individuals to capture footage in real time and instantly post that footage to a social media platform that has the potential to go viral and be seen by millions.

The technological advances that America has seen in the last ten years present enormous opportunities, but also significant challenges. While Twitter and other social media platforms have been used to generate interest in activism and engagement in critical social issues; these platforms have sparked negative behavior in communication. The online comments that emerge from these headlines are abusive, derogatory, and make civil discourse nearly impossible to achieve.

Digital interconnection helps and hurts the church. It helps by giving the church a platform to the wider world to spread the message of Jesus Christ. It can potentially hurt the church through calloused and insensitive statements made by those within the congregation about cultural and political issues that are affecting the sociopolitical landscape of America.

For example, during the series of racialized crises that occurred in the summer of 2016, social media platforms turned into minefields. Dozens of members from my own church took to social media to air out their frustrations with the American criminal justice system and presidential candidate Trump, while others railed against the lazy, disrespectful, and violent black community.

Technology, if not put in its proper place, can rob us of the ability to listen with empathy. It steals intentionality and vulnerability. If the church is to be a vibrant community filled with flawed people, it must acknowledge the potential pitfalls and perils of taking to social media to air out opinions during heated moments that affect our sociopolitical landscape.

These events and people have all, in their own unique way, changed the sociopolitical climate, and one of the results has been that race relations are at their lowest point in decades. Americans now wonder if the race relations will ever get better. The church must act to mitigate the growing tension. However, if any mitigation and proactive measures are to be undertaken, a greater awareness of America's changing sociopolitical climate must happen among America's church leaders. Awareness of any issue can be difficult to achieve, as there are always competing priorities in any institution.

The goal of the realization phase is to help the congregation grow in their awareness of deteriorating race relations in America. To solve any problem, one must first realize that a problem exists. Faith leaders should engage in specific mitigation activities to enable congregations to better respond to help communities recover from racialized storms; to do that, church leaders must better understand America's racial fault lines.

For white church leaders, this understanding can be elusive. Greg Boyd writes, "I believe most white folks genuinely despise racism, so far as they understand it, and sincerely believe they are anti-racist, so far as they understand it. It's just that they don't understand it very far. Our awareness is stunted because our life experience tends to blind us to racism as a subversive structural issue."[xliii] Awareness is pivotal for effective leadership during times of racial crisis. There must be a compelling narrative that church leaders use to motivate their congregation to be forward-thinking and proactive on closing the racial divide in America. Brenda Salter McNeil's book, *Roadmap to Reconciliation* highlights the importance of realization. "The realization phase of the journey involves more than cognitive understanding…it's a state of awareness that requires a response because it literally changes everything we thought we understood about an experience." Faith leaders must cultivate an awareness that is salient, weighty, and challenges people to respond.

can be physical (in the form of infrastructure damage and people being hurt from rioting), but most often is manifested in psychological and sociological ways. The storm surge of division overwhelms schools, churches, government offices, corporations, etc. The winds of hate blow through communities, inciting violence. The rain of rage drenches social media sites all over America. Videos of these killings trend on Facebook, Twitter, and YouTube, giving tens of millions instant access to the tragic moments before a life is taken. Like Hurricane Katrina, these racialized crises have produced psychological scars that have Americans wondering if the country's racial divide will ever heal.[xlix]

Similar to the powerful storm surge that occurs when a hurricane bears down on a coast, racialized crises generate a surge of uproar that can potentially bring a major city to a grinding halt. Baltimore was under curfew for several days during the heat of its unrest when twenty-five-year-old Freddie Gray was killed by police officers. It is estimated that over nine million dollars of damage was done in the city, with one hundred and forty-four vehicles and fifteen buildings burned, and two hundred and fifty-four businesses reporting that they incurred damage and disruption.[1] As hurricanes typically produce sustained winds in excess of one hundred mph, racialized crises generate a sustained rage that disrupts the physical, social, and psychological aspect of individuals and communities in a city.

For many, these race quakes seem insurmountable and overwhelming. They are highly complex, historically rooted, and culturally polarizing events that touch deeply embedded nerves and fears, especially of discrimination and police brutality, particularly in people of color. The uproar and rage is often produced when the tectonic plate of individual experiences of racial prejudice clashes with America's history of white supremacy, particularly manifested in the form of police brutality. Nearly fifty-five years ago Dr. Martin Luther King, Jr. spoke of the terrors that blacks endured at the hands of police.

> "There are those who are asking the devotees of civil rights, 'When will you be satisfied?'" said Martin Luther King, Jr. in his iconic "I Have a Dream" speech at the 1963 march. His words continue to resonate today after a long history of violent confrontations between African-American citizens and the police. "We can never be satisfied as long as the Negro is the victim of the unspeakable horrors of police brutality."[li]

Today, blacks make up close to 13% of the U.S. population, but account for "24% of those fatally shot and killed by the police."[lii] Nearly one hundred years ago, the Illinois Association for Criminal Justice issued the Illinois Crime Survey. This survey, conducted between 1927 and 1928, provided pertinent data on police killings,[liii] finding that "although African Americans made up just 5% of the area's population, they constituted 30% of the victims of police killings."[liv] Sadly, history seems to be repeating itself. The long and painful history of police brutality and state-sanctioned violence against African Americans has created a collective stressor among the African American population. Due to a changing sociopolitical in America, I predict that the number and severity of racialized crises will increase drastically in the next five to ten years. The church must prepare for these disasters by engaging in long-term planning that will enable them to better respond and lead.

III

The Ineffectiveness of the Church

We need to begin to see our communities right now as trauma patients, as a hurt one lying on the mat. We are in a critical state. We must understand that the initial effort in trauma and in critical care situations is to bring some stability. Protests and street rallies express frustration, grief, a sense of insecurity and fear in the face of recurring practices and systems in which people feel susceptible to victimization. A just society is to be judged by how well it treats the weakest, poorest, and most pained of its members. The church specifically must remain answerable to a similar critique.

—F. WILLIS JOHNSON, *HOLDING UP YOUR CORNER*

A majority of Americans now believe that America's race relations have grown worse in the last several years. This perception is ironic given the euphoria around the election of Barack Obama, America's first black president in 2008. At that time, pundits, papers, and people everywhere claimed that the election of America's first black president would usher in a new era of a post-racial society.[lv]

The Ideology of Colorblindness

This post-racial society would dogmatically adhere to the notion of colorblindness. This colorblindness would essentially be a public sightlessness concerning matters of race. Ian Haney López observes in *Dog Whistle Politics: How Coded Racial Appeals Have Reinvented Racism and Wrecked the Middle Class* that colorblindness "holds broad attraction across the political spectrum."[lvi] People who ascribe to this worldview believe that it is critical to solving the problem of racism in America. Acclaimed race theorist, author, and activist, Austin Channing Brown writes:

> It seems many still believe colorblindness is the key to solving racism. Believing in the notion of colorblindness sounds like this, "I don't even see color," or this, "But we are all the same," or this, "I've never looked at you as a (fill in the blank)." These statements are usually followed by a sugary example of our sameness and end with a quote by Martin Luther King, Jr. about character not color being what REALLY counts. And it all sounds pretty good, until you run into someone who refuses to let you forget their race, "If you can't see color, you can't see me."[lvii]

The ideology of colorblindness seeks to downplay the significance of race in the American consciousness. Kendra Hadiya Barber in "What Happened to All the Protests?" identifies three guidelines that inform the ideology of colorblindness: "Race is reduced to pigmentation and is removed from social status, history, and power; noticing race is the same as subscribing to biological differences; and racism is a personal problem that is a result of bigoted individuals rather than a system of power."[lviii] It is important to remember that colorblind ideology is a white-centered ideology. Black and brown people do not have the luxury and privilege to not to see race. The United States' legal and political system was created through the logics of white supremacy which was historically used to dehumanize black and brown people.

Where did colorblind thinking originate? Clearly, the United States has had a long and troubled history regarding race relations. Robert T. Carter notes that over the last several decades the expression of racism has drastically changed in America and that

> ...Over time racism has changed and become more symbolic, subtle, and hidden within the guise of non-prejudicial or nonracist behavior, thought, and justification...Strong negative feelings toward people of Color operate on the subconscious level of awareness. While they [hostile feelings toward people of Color] are often not communicated as open hostility, such feelings and beliefs exist and manifest themselves in colorblind beliefs and practices, as well as by expressions of discomfort, disgust, and fear.[lix]

person's ability to live wholly and abundantly."[lxiii] White faith leaders often find themselves at a loss for words when these crises occur because many of them have bought into the lie that colorblindness is an effective way to deal with America's race problem. The shaking from these race quakes is severe because white Americans are abruptly jolted out of their constructed reality of colorblindness and an individual work ethic as a key to success in life.

In "Color-Blind Racism, Color-Blind Theology, and Church Practices," Mark Hearn makes the point that this type of rationale hinders racial progress and equity. He states that such ideology is a manifestation of a new type of racism and "it occurs when individuals, institutions, and ideologies perpetuate racial inequality by refusing to recognize color in persons but rather see them as non-colorized individuals."[lxiv] He contends that buying into the notion of colorblindness effectively eliminates color and thus a person of color's experiences "in a society where color has historically mattered in terms of physical, social, economic, and spiritual well-being."[lxv] Color matters in our society and if we choose to overlook its salience than we do it at our own peril.

Pastors and faith leaders need an alternative to colorblindness to properly address racialized crises. Austin Channing Brown argues that an effective alternative to colorblindness is to be color conscious. She states:

> Color consciousness is to be aware of race, to no longer disregard it as meaningless or minute. People who are color conscious are comfortable noticing difference without ascribing superiority and inferiority to those differences. They can appreciate cultural differences

> and the diversity of thought, perspective and experience
> that race brings to the world. Color conscious people
> refuse to ignore race because they are too busy exploring
> it for all its beauty, quirkiness, and yes, messiness.[lxvi]

Appreciating cultural differences and the belief that diversity and inclusion makes an institution (especially a church) stronger is paramount to rejecting colorblindness and situates white churches in a better position to respond to racial uproar.

Cultural Lens of White Christians

This book, so far, has covered key elements that are changing the sociopolitical climate in America, what racialized crises are, and the social unrest that they generate. However, why do these crises affect the American Christian church? There are several reasons; chief among them are white Christian's inability and/or unwillingness to acknowledge the ramifications of centuries of structural racism, the fact that systemic racism is present in today's twenty-first century society, and a historic apathy to work for black equality. I plan to use the terms institutional racism, systemic racism, and structural inequality interchangeably throughout this chapter.

First, a breakdown of the term racism. Joseph R. Barndt gives a succinct description of racism, stating that it "is prejudice with power."[lxvii] Systemic racism is essentially institutional arrangements that have historically put people of color at a disadvantage.[lxviii] These institutional measures include the structure of a variety of organizations, including governments, corporations, and social arrangements. These structures have a cumulative and compounding effects of an array of societal factors, including history, culture, ideology of institutions and policies that systematically privilege white people."[lxix]

There are a variety reasons of why some whites struggle to comprehend the structural side of racism, but two are particularly noteworthy. The first is the linguistic shift in the meaning of "racism." The second is the cultural lens that whites use to construct their social reality. The legal barriers that were broken during the American Civil Rights Movement and changing attitudes on race relations has led many to believe that racism (as it existed during the Jim Crow era) is finished. Frederick Harris and Robert Lieberman write on this false perception of victory in "Racial Inequality After Racism: How Institutions Hold Back African Americans" that: "White Americans generally assume that the end of state-sponsored segregation and the legal prohibition of discrimination removed structural barriers to African American advancement."[lxx] This perception is coupled with a successful effort on the part of white authorities to redefine the term racism. Carol Anderson writes on the changing meaning of racism:

> Confronted with civil rights headlines depicting unflattering portrayals of KKK rallies and jackbooted sheriffs, white authority transformed those damning images of white supremacy into the sole definition of racism. This simple but wickedly brilliant conception and linguistic shift served multiple purposes. First and foremost, it was conscience soothing. The whittling down of racism to sheet-wearing goons allowed a cloud of racial innocence to cover many whites who, although "resentful of black progress" and determined to ensure

that racial inequality remained untouched, could see and project themselves as the "kind of upstanding white citizen[s]" who were "positively outraged at the tactics of the Ku Klux Klan." The focus on the Klan also helped to designate racism as an individual aberration rather than something systemic, institutional, and pervasive.[lxxi]

The linguistic shift of the term racism has proved to be exceptionally problematic in securing racial justice and ameliorating the gross racial inequities in our society. How can one seek to solve a problem that a majority of white Americans believe doesn't exist? It was virtually impossible to deny the structural racism that existed during the Jim Crow era. White supremacy was pervasive and easily observable. Today, most white Americans believe that blacks are to blame for the persistent problems that exist in their community. Harris and Lieberman write: "In a 2013 Gallup poll, for instance, 83% of white Americans said that factors other than discrimination were to blame for African Americans' lower levels of employment, lower incomes, and lower-quality housing."[lxxii]

The inability of white Americans to acknowledge structural racism is a topic that is covered extensively by sociologists Michael Emerson and Christian Smith in their book, *Divided by Faith: Evangelical Religion and the Problem of Race in America*. This groundbreaking work is an extensive ethnographic project that surveys well over two thousand white Christians on their perceptions on race. It provides an in-depth analysis into the psychology and philosophy of white Christians in America. Emerson and Smith make the claim that white Christians further exacerbate the problems of racial inequality because of the cultural lens they use to construct their social reality.[lxxiii]

The cultural lenses that they employ are accountable free-will individualism, relationalism, and anti-structuralism—lenses that unfortunately leave them blind to the pervasive problems that the African American community faces and also produce a lack of urgency to intervene to ameliorate the issues the black community faces. The anti-structuralism lens is described as the "ability to perceive or unwillingness to accept social structural influences."[lxxiv] Emerson and Smith state that whites find systemic justification for inequities wrongheaded and believe that highlighting structural explanations for racial inequalities merely shifts the blame.[lxxv]

Racialized crises affect the church in a negative way because of the ideology of hyper-individualism. This belief, which is a strong current in the American sociopolitical river, blinds white Christians to the ramifications of social structures that produce inequality and encourages them to lay blame at the feet of the marginalized. Barber writes, "With racism allegedly gone, anyone can pull themselves up by their bootstraps, and any racial inequalities that still exist are due to a lack of motivation on behalf of blacks." Injustice and inequality is rationalized and permitted to continue under the guise of a lack of an individual effort on the part of blacks. Emerson and Smith comment on this pervasive individualism,

> As carpenters are limited to building with the tools in their kits (hammers encourage the use of nails, drills encourage the use of screws), so white evangelicals are severely constrained by their religion-cultural tools.

> Although much in Christian scripture and tradition point to the influence of social structures on individuals, the stress on individualism has been so complete for such a long time in white American evangelical culture that such tools are nearly unavailable.[lxxvi]

Individualism is an idol in the American Christian church that makes good-hearted Christians deaf to the cries of communities on the margins, numb to the communal pain that is generated during racialized tragedies, and blind to the social structures that support and perpetuate inequalities and injustice.

Psychological, Psychosocial, and Physiological Distress

Like susceptible coastal communities in America's Gulf region, the church's credibility and witness is vulnerable to the severity of racialized crises. During the summer of 2016, I witnessed the pain, confusion, and fear of numerous people within my own congregation (especially minorities), whose souls were being shaken by these storms. I remember feeling incredibly vulnerable during this time while I was serving as a pastor in a majority white church.

In the case of Mike Brown and the subsequent mass social unrest that occurred in America, an enormous amount of emotional injury was experienced throughout the country. Immense psychological stress is often generated simultaneously, communally and individually, among African Americans from tragedies like shootings of unarmed black men and women. Faith leaders would be wise to both recognize and mitigate on the psychological element from racialized tragedies. If the church is to truly be a healing place for a hurting world then it must take the lead in truth finding and reconciliation. It must become a place where deep psychological and emotional wounds that congregants suffer from racialized storms can be addressed, rehabilitated, and healed. Recent scholarship has shown that racial discrimination has physiological and mental health impacts.

According to Robert T. Carter, "Racial stressors have been found, in a variety of studies, to produce physical outcomes such as high blood pressure, risk for heart disease, and increased vulnerability to a variety of negative health outcomes that can contribute to greater psychological and emotional distress."[lxxvii] These stressors aren't limited to individual racist events, but can be generated from the racialized storms that strike the sociopolitical landscape in America.

> A stressor does not require physical contact for it to be severe or traumatizing. Instead, the case for the concept of race-based trauma is that it provides a more precise description of the psychological consequences of interpersonal or institutional traumas motivated by the devaluing of one's race...It is theorized that race-based traumatic stressors have the potential to affect victims cognitively, affectively, somatically, relationally, behaviorally, and spiritually (Bryant-Davis & Ocampo, 2005). Cognitive effects may include difficulty concentrating, remembering, and focusing. Affective effects may include numbness, depression, anxiety, grief, and anger. Somatic complaints may include migraines, nausea, and body aches. Relationally, victims may demonstrate distrust of members of the dominant group or, in cases of internalized racism,

distrust of members of their racial group. Behaviorally, victims may begin to self-medicate through substance misuse or other self-harming activities. Spiritually, victims may question their faith in God, humanity, or both. There has been evidence of race-based traumatic stress resulting in intrusive thoughts, hyper-vigilance, and avoidance.[lxxviii]

When you compound the severity of stress that is produced from racialized crises with the cumulative psychological burden from daily and weekly mini-traumas (micro aggressions), the effects can be devastating. Tim Wise, in *Colorblind: The Rise of Post-Racial Politics and the Retreat from Racial Equity*, highlights hundreds of studies that show a connection between racial discrimination and harmful health outcomes that people of color experience. He writes that, "racial discrimination increases stress levels among persons of color, thereby elevating blood pressure and correlating directly with worse health."[lxxix] Why do traumatic events hurt the church? Because these events produce a collective trauma among people of color through self-identification and shared experiences of the discriminatory event.

Medical studies have revealed that the "evidence supports the anecdotal notion, that ambiguous interpersonal interactions that are perceived as being racially motivated may confer more profound emotional and physical health consequences."[lxxx] These racist incidents (which I believe include racialized crises that generate enormous sociopolitical unrest in the sociocultural landscape in America) can contribute to "negative psychological, psychosocial, and physiological effects."[lxxxi]

It is vital that faith leaders recognize that many people of color internalize the racist incidents they experience and acknowledge this. "Healing the wounds of race-based trauma requires acknowledging them nationally and globally."[lxxxii] This internalization accumulates over time and can not only lead to negative physiological outcomes, but coupled with the stress of a crises can lead to emotional issues such as isolation, depression, and intense anger. These stressors are not just limited to a certain locale. Exposure to the unrest can lead to pain anywhere the events can be viewed in the media. Contemporary Christian leaders must think systematically and recognize that people grieve, not because of a singular discriminatory offense, but because that offense is associated and compounded with a whole history of prejudice and oppression. It is the darker side to American history and the present-day trauma of discrimination. Such trauma includes,

> being denied promotions, home mortgages, or business loans; being a target of a security guard; or being stopped in traffic...a pattern of racist events forms across the life domains of minority citizens. This pervasive pattern requires ongoing coping and expenditures of psychic energy.[lxxxiii]

It is necessary to understand the weight of historical injustice and its sociopolitical implications on people of color. The historical injustices that have happened in America have produced a generational and tribal pain for many African Americans. The impact of slavery, reconstruction, and Jim Crow are not far removed from the consciousness of our nation. The harmful effects of systemic racism in our society continue to produce immense economic, educational, social inequities.

Racialized crises exacerbate this sense of mourning because of self-identification to the tragedy, shared discriminatory experiences, and injustices that African Americans have experienced historically in America. Christena Cleveland writes about the phenomena of psychological homelessness that affects people of color in predominately white churches, Christian colleges, and seminaries.

> Many people of color who attend predominantly white churches and Christian colleges/seminaries talk about feeling explicitly welcomed by the majority group but implicitly excluded. On the surface (and for the most part), members of the well-intentioned white majority are REALLY, REALLY nice to them. People of color are greeted warmly in the hallways, on the bike path, and in the pews. They are explicitly told that they are welcome at the church or school. They are even invited into the homes of colleagues, classmates, and fellow church members. However, despite these welcoming individual actions, people of color often report that their experience at these Christian organizations is marked by feelings of loneliness, marginalization, exclusion, and misunderstanding. This response both befuddles and discourages the well-intentioned white people and leads people of color to experience a seemingly unshakeable feeling of what theologian Miroslav Volf calls "psychological homelessness." They feel out of place, on the edge of the circle, disconnected from the life-giving heartbeat of the community.[lxxxiv]

I can attest to this feeling. While I grew up in the black church, I have worshipped at predominately white churches since I was a college freshman. I remember the first time I felt psychologically homeless from a racialized event. The election of Barack Obama to the presidency in 2008 elicited a range of emotions among white Christians in my context, ranging from elation to despair. There were racial undertones in many conversations. For example, one of my white Christian sisters stated, "I can't believe we are considering electing a guy with the middle name Hussein to the presidency." Another white friend who was fearful of the country's economic outlook said, "I just think that he [Obama] is going to take all the good jobs and give them to black people." I often remember being befuddled and uncomfortable in these conversations. Because I was the minority in the room and in the conversation, I often felt insecure about giving my opinion.

During President Obama's second term, several racialized crises struck America's sociopolitical landscape. Trayvon Martin's murder in 2012, Michael Brown's murder in 2014, the rise of the Black Lives Matter social movement, the removal of the Confederate Battle flag on the South Carolina State Grounds were events that were challenging to navigate as a black pastor in a predominantly white church. When these events were making nationals headlines and eliciting negative reactions from the white community, rarely was anything acknowledged on Sunday morning or during church leadership meetings. The feeling of isolation and loneliness intensified for me when these crises occurred. One of the privileges of being white is to not have to pay attention to cultural issues that affect black and brown life. Adams writes:

> White churches are hard for black people because many
> people do not understand the black experience to be

both corporate and individual. Black people share many common experiences, and these experiences build a unique solidarity among us. This is why a racial injustice in Florida can shake black people in Washington State. But often folks think that means that every black person feels the same way about every issue, which isn't the case.[lxxxv]

The pain that people of color feel during racialized storms produces a communal mourning. It's a very real wound that hurts and is tied to systemic and historic injustice. President Barack Obama addressed the nation after a series of racialized crises during the summer of 2016:

> I know that Americans are struggling right now with what we've witnessed over the past week [7/5/16–7/11/16]. First the shooting in Minnesota and Baton Rouge...Then the targeting of police by the shooter here an act not just of demented violence but of racial hatred. All of it's left us wounded and angry and hurt. It's as if the deepest fault lines of our democracy have suddenly been exposed; perhaps even widened. And although we know that such divisions are not new, though they surely have been worse in even the recent past that offers us little comfort. Faced with this violence we wonder if the divides of race in America can ever be breached; we wonder if an African American community that feels unfairly targeted by police and police departments that feel unfairly maligned for doing their jobs can ever understand each other's experiences. We turn on the tv or surf the internet and we can watch positions harden and lines drawn and people retreat to their respective corners...We see all of this and it's hard not to think that the center won't hold and that things might get worse.[lxxxvi]

Hurricane Katrina taught scholars and practitioners numerous lessons. In some ways, during Katrina, we rallied together with help pouring in from all over the nation, but in other ways we were deeply divided in our narratives as we tried to explain the causes of the catastrophic conditions that occurred. Kanye West's statement, "George Bush doesn't care about black people," reflected a deep sentiment of people of color across the nation as they watched poor black bodies floating in the floodwaters of New Orleans[lxxxvii]—a sentiment that blamed governmental and social inaction for continued pain and hardship. The lesson for churches is the same—there are dead bodies in the water when these racialized crises strike—victims of psychological and emotional trauma—and the church must not be characterized by inaction and ineptitude.

The psychological, psychosocial, and physiological effects from racialized storms are not randomized—whimsically impacting different groups of people—but are socially structured along lines of race. It is imperative that predominately white churches *realize* the degree of social vulnerability that people of color face during the onslaught of these storms. They are more prone to psychosocial and emotional pain. People of all colors and cultures face varying degrees of discrimination and distress. However, when taking into account America's historical legacy of enslavement and oppression of African Americans, it is logical to deduce that there is an extreme sensitivity that African American possesses in regard to racialized tragedies in America.

Racialized crises hurt the church because churches fail to realize how the general patterns of oppression and marginalization of African American communities play out on a daily basis during non-disaster times. The ignorance makes these crises more severe, because anger and resentment is stockpiled in the souls of blacks. The flood of rage that flows from daily injustices has the potential to undo any work on racial reconciliation and healing that churches undertake.

It starts with realization. Realizing that there have been and continue to be significant elements in our cultural landscape that are leading to sociopolitical climate change. It begins with realizing that the death of Michael Brown, Philando Castile, Alton Sterling, Ahmuad Arbery, Breonna Taylor, and the subsequent uproar that was produced are not isolated events. It begins when we realize that these tragedies are like storms that flood and overwhelm people's lives. The disruption that these events bring is profound and disproportionately affects people of color. It starts with realizing that these racialized storms hurt the church's credibility, hinders racially progress when there is silence in the pulpit.

Why Realization Matters?

Before an adequate response can be given, sound preparation must be undertaken. Preparation is key. Crises are inevitable in life. "Individuals may suffer the loss of loved ones, health, homes, financial stability, social support, sense of stability, and other resources important to daily living. Those impacted demonstrate a wide range of psychological reactivity ranging from brief, transient distress to long-term psychopathology."[lxxxviii] Racialized storms are crises that disrupt the sociopolitical landscape of our country, city, and communities. These storms also cause crises in individuals. These are inevitably accompanied by a degree of psychological distress. Coping with the experience of loss and pressure demands emotional energy.

The term "crisis" refers essentially to an unexpected circumstance. "A crisis marks a phase of disorder in the development of a person, an organization, a community, an ecosystem, a business sector, or a polity."[lxxxix] While not every crisis can be foreseen, we can learn from the past to become more resilient for the future.

It's vital that the church fully comprehend the *why* behind resilience building. If congregations don't realize the necessity of mitigating disruption from racialized storms, they will eventually lose sight and interest in taking proactive measures to reduce the severity of these storms. Simon Sinek explains:

> People don't buy what you do, they buy why you do it. The problem is that organizations use the tangible features and benefits to go to a rational argument for why the company, product or idea is better than another...Why does Apple have such a disproportionate level of success? Why are they more innovative? Why are they consistently more profitable? And how did they manage to build such a cultish loyal following— something very few companies ever are able to achieve?[xc]

The reason, Sinek argues, is that Apple leads with their *why*. Faith leaders must do the same when it comes to fostering readiness in the face of racialized storms. L. Gregory Jones writes about Sinek in his book, *Christian Social Innovation*:

Sinek delivered a TED talk in 2009 that has been viewed more than twenty-five million times. It is called "Start with Why." He contends that most people and most organizations start with a rational explanation of what they do and how they do it. People are typically very clear about what they do, and often somewhat clear about how they do it. But they tend to be fuzziest about why they do what they do. The best leaders and organizations, Sinek argues, reverse that order: they are clearest about their purpose, their why, and that leads them to explain how they accomplish their purpose and what they do to further those accomplishments.[xci]

If congregations truly desire to be more ready and responsive to racialized crises then they must truly grasp the why—which is what the Realization phase attempts to explain. Salter-McNeil writes that "the work of the preparation phase begins with capacity building. This is where we determine what capabilities, resources, strengths, training and so on we need to help us move forward. This phase is about preparing for action that is not based in reaction."[xcii] Difficult choices must be made to prepare for these storms. However, the benefits outweigh the initial cost.

Faith leaders need to foster an awareness of the advantages of preparing for racialized crises. This starts with Christian leaders fully comprehending how significant the issue of race is in America. Once this realization is achieved, faith leaders need to engage in the work of bringing that awareness to their context. Doing this enables churches to become resilient in the wake of sociopolitical unrest from racialized storms. Resilience is key. Judith Rodin writes:

> Resilience is the capacity of any entity—an individual, a community, an organization, or a natural system—to prepare for disruptions, to recover from shocks and stresses, and to adapt and grow from a disruptive experience...As you build resilience, therefore, you become more able to prevent or mitigate stresses and shocks you can identify and better able to respond to those you can't predict or avoid.[xciii]

It is paramount to understand that anyone can engage in the work of resilience through mitigation and adaptation. This concept is not restricted to public policy officials or emergency managers. Everyone can achieve enhanced resilience in some form. We cannot predict the situations in life that will force us to spend money. However, we can control how we prepare for uncertainties. The same can be said for enhancing a church's capacity to respond to racialized crises.

> One way to reduce the impacts of disasters on the nation and its communities is to invest in enhancing resilience...Enhanced resilience allows better anticipation of disasters and better planning to reduce disaster losses—rather than waiting for an event to occur and paying for it afterward. However, building the culture and practice of disaster resilience is not simple or inexpensive. Decisions about how and when to invest in increasing resilience involve short- and long-term planning and investments of time and resources prior to an event. Although the resilience of individuals and communities may be readily recognized after a disaster, resilience is currently rarely acknowledged before a disaster takes a place, making the payoff for resilience investments challenging for individuals, communities.[xciv]

Resilience building is not a simple task. The work of prevention is arduous. It requires bringing public awareness to an issue that might not seem important at the time is often highly polarizing. It requires a rigorous educative process to be conversant about issues that affect race relations in America.

> Building resilience creates two aspects of benefits: it enables individuals, communities, and organizations to better withstand a disruption more effectively, and it enables them to improve their current systems and situations. But also enables them to build new relationships, take on new endeavors and initiatives, and reach out for new opportunities, ones that may never have been imagined before.[xcv]

Resilience building through mitigation and adaptation involves foresight to see the long-term advantages despite the short-term struggles. The goal is for resilience thinking to be a part of a broader organizational strategy regarding the preparation for racialized crises.

PART TWO

READINESS

Institutional Mitigation of Racialized Tragedies

REALIZATION

RENEWAL

RACIAL CRISIS
FRAMEWORK

READINESS

RESPONSIVENESS

The second stage in the Racial Crises Framework is readiness. Here, I focus on specific actions a church can take to prepare for racialized traumatic events. Salter-McNeil writes that churches and leaders "fail to realize that relational connections cannot be sustained without structural intentionality. Structures to support our efforts toward long-term reconciliation have to be established."[xcvi] Readiness is critical to an effective response. A pastor whose church has taken proactive measures to prepare for racialized crises and is actively engaged in racial reconciliation will be far more adept at navigating sociopolitical distress generated by a crises than a pastor who has done nothing to combat the prejudice and bigotry that resides in his/her congregation and community.

The key is to become proactive rather than reactive. Unfortunately, white Christian leaders were caught flatfooted when riots broke out in Baltimore after the death of Freddie Gray. When Eric Garner was choked to death in New York City and tens of thousands took to the streets in New York to protest, too many faith leaders remained silent. Being proactive, in a state of readiness, is vital to leading your congregation and community through a racialized crises.

Judith Rodin writes about the impact that readiness can play in an institution's response to a catastrophe. She emphasizes the United States Coast Guard's successful response to Hurricane Katrina was successful because of key steps that were taken before the storm hit.

> When Hurricane Katrina hit the Gulf Coast in 2005 and caused a series of cascading disruptions—flood, collapse, loss of essential services including utilities, sanitation, communication—the U.S. Coast Guard (USCG) was ready. It was one of the Coast Guard's largest search and rescue missions ever...Of the 60,000 people who were unable to escape the floodwaters—they fled to their rooftops or were stranded on isolated patches of high ground—the Coast Guard rescued more than 33,500...The Coast Guard was able to conduct such a successful response for many reasons, among them preparedness and effective governance. Before the storm made landfall, the Coast Guard moved its command and control posts away from the hurricane's path, so it would not be rendered dysfunctional...The Coast Guard was highly aware of the danger that official responders face in a crisis and of the fact that they cannot offer an effective response if they have been made dysfunctional themselves...The actions taken by

the Coast Guard before the storm became a crisis were
planned and practiced with such regularity that, when
it came time to respond, service members from New
Orleans to New England knew what they were expected
to do, were ready to do it and, in the event, did it.[xcvii]

The Coast Guard's effective response to Hurricane Katrina is
a key example of how institutional preparedness can make a
profound difference in responding to a crisis. In many ways,
the church is like a hospital. People who are emotionally
devastated and in distress walk through the church's doors
every Sunday.

In times of national crisis, people are searching for
answers and comfort. The church has the potential to be a
healing place for those who are hurting from the pain of
racialized storms. However, for this to happen, Christian
leaders must first realize how destructive racialized storms
are, then ready themselves and their leadership team to
rescue those who are drowning in the floodwaters of
loneliness, fear, and anxiety.

IV

The Need for Awareness

The education of white theologians did not prepare them to deal with Watts, Detroit, and Newark. What was needed was a new way of looking at theology that must emerge out of the dialectic of black history and culture.

—JAMES CONE, *GOD OF THE OPPRESSED*

Michael Eric Dyson writes about the need for greater racial literacy in his book *Tears We Cannot Stop*.[xcviii] He argues that to achieve racial equality, whites must educate themselves on issues that affect black and brown culture. Education on the racial inequities and structural racism that exists today in America is pivotal to bridging the racial divide. A better understanding of the disruption that racialized crises cause will compel faith leaders to be more intentional in shepherding their congregations during times of social unrest. Church leaders must become more racially literate if they seek to close the racial divide that exists in their congregations and communities. Similarly, one of the major recommendations of my final project on climate change adaptation in the Houston-Galveston region was an emphasis on educating constituents:

> Along with rebranding, H-GAC should be involved in providing education, information, and facts to constituents in support of their planning processes. By providing communities with facts, H-GAC will give community leaders and managers the tools and knowledge that is needed to provide the proper protection to their citizens. Included in this should be education about adaptation systems and resiliency projects that communities can implement during disaster recovery.[xcix]

Likewise, faith leaders will be overwhelmed by the process of mitigation if they are not educated.

This discussion of realization, while not an exhaustive study on race, does offer foundational elements for better understanding the race quakes that have shaken America during the last eight years. We can prepare for these events in a more informed and intentional way by educating ourselves on why these crises generate so much distress in communities of color and why it's so difficult for white people to talk about it. No one knows when another Charlottesville or Ahmaud Arbery will happen, but if pastors become educated on matters of race in America, they can put themselves in a better position to respond and lead during times of national crisis.

The Story of Joseph

Joseph's ascent to second-in-command of Egypt in the Genesis narrative is a remarkable story of God's providence and unique timing. This popular biblical account is an inspiring tale of perseverance, forgiveness, and patience. In addition to the aforementioned virtues, this narrative illustrates a classical example of climate change adaptation. Genesis 41:17–24 recounts Pharaoh's approaching Joseph with the hopes that he can interpret a harrowing and perplexing dream:

> So Pharaoh told Joseph his dream. "In my dream," he said, "I was standing on the bank of the Nile River, and I saw seven fat, healthy cows come up out of the river and begin grazing in the marsh grass. But then I saw seven sick-looking cows, scrawny and thin, come up after them. I've never seen such sorry-looking animals in all the land of Egypt. These thin, scrawny cows ate the seven fat cows. But afterward you wouldn't have known it, for they were still as thin and scrawny as before! Then I woke up. In my dream I also saw seven heads of grain, full and beautiful, growing on a single stalk. Then seven more heads of grain appeared, but

> these were blighted, shriveled, and withered by the east wind. And the shriveled heads swallowed the seven healthy heads. I told these dreams to the magicians, but no one could tell me what they mean."[c]

Verse 8 gives insight into Pharaoh's emotional state: "The next morning Pharaoh was very disturbed by the dreams." The key word here is "disturbed." Adaptation and mitigation of racialized storms will not be undertaken unless the higher levels of leadership in an organization are disturbed. Action is typically not taken until disruption knocks on our door. Pharaoh quickly acted by calling in magicians and wise men of Egypt to interpret his dreams.

Pharaoh's actions present an example of realization. Pharaoh became aware of a potential problem through the emotional disturbance of a dream and subsequently engaged in sense-making. The authors of *The Politics of Crisis Management* describe sense-making as a way to collect and process information "that will help crisis managers to detect an emerging crisis and understand the significance of what is going on during a crisis."[ci] While the famine had not yet occurred, the dreams that Pharaoh experienced were significant enough for him to seek help in processing what they meant. Pharaoh's sense-making resulted in Joseph being summoned and eventually interpreting his dreams. Sense-making is an important part of the realization phase.

> It is very difficult to predict crises. But it is possible to detect an emerging crisis in time to shift the course of events in a more favorable direction. Early detection means faster deployment of resources, which, in turn, can save lives. But all too often, escalating crises come as a complete surprise to leaders...Once a crisis

becomes manifest, crisis responders will want to understand what is happening in order to take effective measures to deal with the consequences. They must assess how threatening and urgent the events are, to what or whom, and consider how the situation might develop in the period to come.[cii]

Joseph detected the crisis and proposed a plan that would reduce the severity of the calamitous famine that was to set to affect Egypt and its neighbors. His plan essentially shifted the course of events in a favorable direction for the inhabitants of Egypt and surrounding regions.

> Joseph responded, "Both of Pharaoh's dreams mean the same thing. God is telling Pharaoh in advance what he is about to do. The seven healthy cows and the seven healthy heads of grain both represent seven years of prosperity. The seven thin, scrawny cows that came up later and the seven thin heads of grain, withered by the east wind, represent seven years of famine. This will happen just as I have described it, for God has revealed to Pharaoh in advance what he is about to do. The next seven years will be a period of great prosperity throughout the land of Egypt. But afterward there will be seven years of famine so great that all the prosperity will be forgotten in Egypt. Famine will destroy the land. This famine will be so severe that even the memory of the good years will be erased. As for having two similar dreams, it means that these events have been decreed by God, and he will soon make them happen."[ciii]

Joseph realized the significance and meaning of Pharaoh's dreams through interpretation. He becomes aware of a potentially catastrophic climatic event. However, Joseph does more than give an interpretation. In Genesis 41:33–36, he proposes a plan to mitigate the effects of the famine:

Therefore, Pharaoh should find an intelligent and wise man and put him in charge of the entire land of Egypt. Then Pharaoh should appoint supervisors over the land and let them collect one-fifth of all the crops during the seven good years. Have them gather all the food produced in the good years that are just ahead and bring it to Pharaoh's storehouses. Store it away, and guard it so there will be food in the cities. That way there will be enough to eat when the seven years of famine come to the land of Egypt. Otherwise this famine will destroy the land.[civ]

In this passage, Joseph shifts from realization to readiness. He becomes aware that the climate will drastically change in a few years. He senses the threat and addresses Egypt's vulnerability by utilizing existing assets to minimize the disruption that the famine would bring. Joseph engages in readiness by essentially creating a community action plan that systematically stockpiled resources and a distribution plan to allocate those resources in an orderly fashion.

Joseph's suggestions were well received by Pharaoh and his officials. So Pharaoh asked his officials, "Can we find anyone else like this man so obviously filled with the spirit of God?" Then Pharaoh said to Joseph, "Since God has revealed the meaning of the dreams to you, clearly no one else is as intelligent or wise as you are. You will be in charge of my court, and all my people will take orders from you. Only I, sitting on my throne, will have a rank higher than yours." Pharaoh said to Joseph, "I hereby put you in charge of the entire land of Egypt." Then Pharaoh removed his signet ring from his hand and placed it on Joseph's finger. He dressed him in fine linen clothing and hung a gold chain around his neck. Then he had Joseph ride in the chariot reserved for his second-in-command. And wherever Joseph went, the command was shouted, "Kneel down!" So Pharaoh put Joseph in charge of all Egypt.[cv]

Genesis 41:37–43 describes Joseph's ascent to power once Pharaoh heard of his wisdom. Joseph saved the Egyptian nation and ensured the survival of the Israelite people through climate change adaptation and natural disaster mitigation. This story illustrates Joseph's prudence and the significance of readiness.

The biblical account in Genesis 41 doesn't specifically mention what caused the change in climate. What it does illustrate is the cataclysmic conditions that the famine had and how Joseph prepared for it. As Judith Rodin writes, "What resilience-building actions can be taken to decrease the impact that disruptions will have?"[cvi]

The church must undergo a paradigm shift that moves beyond the quest for greater numerical diversity in ethnicity, but seeks a radical inclusion that gives people of color a seat at the table and a voice to speak. Racialized storms can make it especially difficult to achieve and sustain diversity. Racialized crises are likely to impede work toward greater diversity in the Body of Christ. Faith leaders need to look beyond racial percentages in their congregations and seek to give a voice to those on the margins.

V

Establishing Readiness Through Climate Change Adaptation and Natural Disaster Mitigation Strategies

Pray if you want, but we need to do something.

—WILL WILLIMON, *WHO LYNCHED WILLIE EARLE?*

The events of the summer of 2016 alerted me to several thought-provoking dilemmas: How should the church respond to these tragedies? What can the church do to comfort its congregants during these storms? What strategies should be implemented to prepare for these tumultuous times? How can the church reduce the psychological distress of its congregants? What steps should the church take to close the sociological, political, and racial gaps that sociopolitical unrest widen? What biblical themes should the church prioritize and communicate during these times?

The purpose of the Racial Crisis Framework is to enable churches to adapt to a changing sociopolitical climate and mitigate the unrest and disruption that individuals, congregations, and communities suffer from racialized storms. The Racial Crisis Framework deploys strategies from the fields of climate change adaptation and natural disaster mitigation. If implemented in a congregational context, these strategies can "reduce the psychological distress among individuals and communities that are exposed to the acute collective stressor" of racialized crises.[cvii] I propose five strategies for mitigating the impact of racialized storms. Together, they provide faith leaders a toolkit to better prepare for and respond to these storms in their congregational context.

These racialized crises, like hurricanes, are inevitable and will continue; hence, it is necessary to invest energy into mitigation and preparation. It is possible to learn from various methods of natural hazard mitigation and discern parallels and implement strategies in a congregational context when we experience sociopolitical crises. Johnny

Bernard Hill notes in *The First Black President*, "Even Obama acknowledged that in many of our urban cities, quiet storms and wars are raging and, if left unattended, will expand to the neatly manicured gated communities of the suburbs and mainstream American life."[cviii]

Climate Change Adaptation and Natural Disaster Mitigation

In this chapter, I analyze strategies from the fields of climate change adaptation and natural disaster mitigation and adapt them to a congregational context to mitigate the disruption from racialized crises. Recent natural disasters, in the past five years, have spurred an emerging interest among individuals and institutions alike to become more resilient. Although "mitigation is a public policy response…it is also an effort that individuals, business, and other institutions can undertake."[cix] Churches can ready themselves to respond to racialized crises, but the key is to focus on long-term planning, to engage in the work of preparation during peace time.

When a racialized crisis strikes, pastors and faith leaders are too often blindsided by the abruptness of anger and the intensity of division that spills out on local and national news and social media platforms. As the winds of tension blow, Christians are left without a way to pacify the pain in their neighborhoods, schools, and workplaces. Preparation during peace time (on the part of faith leaders) will enable and embolden laypeople to be the peacemakers that God intended them to be in a society that is torn apart by categorizations, misunderstandings, and hostility.

The Challenge of Mitigation

Long-term planning and preparation offer many significant benefits to institutions, including churches. However, despite the advantages afforded by mitigation, few individuals and institutions commit to the process. Leaders who expect major crises to occur often engage in proactive measures to mitigate the disruption of that crisis. Recognizing the disruption from these crises is critical to proactive measures being taken. Pastors and faith leaders need to be informed of local and national news, particularly of news that can potentially exacerbate race relations in America. Pastors who take the time and effort to stay updated on present-day issues that affect our sociopolitical landscape and who educate themselves in the history of racial injustice will be more apt to engage in the arduous work of mitigation and sociopolitical adaptation.

Michael Eric Dyson notes the importance of white people educating themselves about black and brown life and culture. He posits that one aspect of white privilege is not ever having to feel the need to be informed about issues that black and brown people face in America.[cx] He advocates for whites to read books that underscore the depth of pain that blacks have suffered from centuries of oppression and discrimination, including the horrors of slavery, racial terrorism, economic and educational inequality, and voter disenfranchisement.

The main challenge to mitigation is that people do not believe that a natural disaster will affect them. Whether they live in tornado alley on the plains of Kansas, on the hurricane-threatened coast of Florida, or along the San Andreas fault line in California, many people go their entire lives without preparing for the impact of a natural disaster. The same ignorance applies to faith leaders and racialized crises. One question I like to ask church leaders is this: If a thousand neo-Nazis and Ku Klux Klan members march in your city, what will you say to your congregation on Sunday morning? If Ahmaud Arbery was murdered in your city, how would you prepare your staff and lead your church in that time of crisis?

Cooperation, Collaboration, Coordination with Community Stakeholders

An important strategy to adapt to the harmful ramifications of climate change and to mitigate the disruption and devastation of natural disasters is to foster cooperation, collaboration, and coordination with institutional actors in a city and community. Judith Rodin quotes Rob Dudgeon (Deputy Director of San Francisco's Department of Emergency Management) on working with various actors to prepare for the next major earthquake. "It's about getting people to work together more than it's about authority...We have to make sure everybody's at the table and work with the various constituencies"[cxi] It is imperative that faith leaders get outside the four walls of the church and build bridges with key community stakeholders in the cities, in order to expose themselves to different opinions and strategies. Congregations need to develop a stronger capacity to cope to an ever-changing sociopolitical climate.

Faith leaders should first identify like-minded institutions to begin the process of building strategic partnerships. Once these are identified, faith leaders need to initiate a process of association with these various constituencies for the mutual benefit of mitigating the impact of racialized storms. Cooperation should eventually lead to collaboration and collaboration should eventually lead to coordination. While all three terms are synonymous, there are important nuances to their definitions. According to Merriam-Webster, cooperation is an "association of persons for common benefit."[cxii] Collaboration is more integrated. Instead of just a loose association, collaboration fosters an amalgamation of ideas and values.

John Spencer contrasts cooperative and collaborative groups. He remarks that "collaboration begins with trust and a shared vision for what you want to accomplish."[cxiii] He then lays out the differences between collaborative and cooperative groups.

> In most cases, we started out as a cooperative group and we shifted into a collaborative group over time. Cooperative groups are more like networks built on respect and shared norms. The work shifts between independence and dependence where the members remain autonomous but agree to share information, tasks, and ideas. By contrast, a collaborative group is interdependent, with a shared vision and values. The mutual respect evolves into trust and the transparency eventually leads to vulnerability.[cxiv]

Spencer then emphasizes eight points that characterize cooperative groups and eight that characterize collaborative groups. These points are presented in the diagram below, where they are contrasted to illustrate the subtle nuances between the two terms.

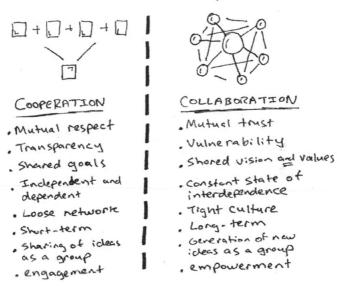

COOPERATIVE V. COLLABORATIVE
By John Spencer @spencerideas

COOPERATION
- Mutual respect
- Transparency
- Shared goals
- Independent and dependent
- Loose network
- Short-term
- Sharing of ideas as a group
- engagement

COLLABORATION
- Mutual trust
- Vulnerability
- Shared vision and values
- Constant state of interdependence
- Tight culture
- Long-term
- Generation of new ideas as a group
- empowerment

cxv

Once mutual trust, shared visions and values, and interdependence have been established between organizations, coordination is the inevitable result. Policies and strategies are executed jointly to maximize impact. "Resources are acknowledged and can be made available for a specific project."cxvi Coordination pools economic, knowledge-based, and material resources toward a "specific project or task."cxvii The process of cooperation, collaboration, and coordination is an important strategy to mitigate the disruption caused by natural disasters. It is also a process that can benefit faith leaders looking to adapt a changing sociopolitical climate.

Cooperation

Cooperation is the first step toward effective mitigation. Organizations looking to build strategic partnership toward a shared goal needn't worry about all their values and interest aligning right off the bat. More important is being exposed to the thought and processes of other groups. That cannot happen if an institution remains within its four walls. Natural disasters force institutional actors to cooperate with one another because no organization is large enough to remedy all the problems that are caused by natural disasters.

When a major hurricane hits a coastal region, a variety of sub-governmental actors are forced to work together to prepare for, respond to, and recover from the storm. Whether the U.S. Coast Guard actively engaged in search and rescue operations or the American Red Cross providing relief through the distribution of food and water to victims, institutions must work together before, during, and after storms.

> For practitioners, cooperation between sub-governmental units is often viewed as an ideal situation that, if achieved, can generate government efficiency, effectiveness, and mutual beneficial outcomes. When change is needed, or perceived to be needed, better cooperation is usually the clarion call.[cxviii]

Cooperation is prevalent among nation-states and sub-governmental units, such as the UN or NATO. The field of Public Administration focuses on how government can be more efficient and effective in managing activities and resources. The book, *Designing Resilience*, describes the view of cooperation dominant among management scholars:

> Management scholars focus on cooperation within and among organizations. They see cooperation as the process by which individuals, groups, and organizations come together, interact, and form psychological relationships for mutual gain or benefit.[cxix]

Again, the focus is how organizations can mutually gain and benefit from forming relationships and loose networks with other organizations. The authors make the case that cooperation leads to trust building, social capital, and greater appreciation for external points of view."[cxx]

Arjen Boin notes that the focus of leadership (when it comes to the crisis management) should be on creating and sustaining key external relationships with other institutions.

> Leaders are important—not only as all powerful deciders but rather as designers, facilitators, and guardians of an institutional arrangement that produces effective decision making and coordination processes at all levels...They should invest in building trusted relationships across organizations, jurisdictions, and communities that are at risk of crisis and help them to develop the social capital and trust that are so crucial in facilitating the emergent, informal, fast, and inclusive coordination processes needed for effective crisis response and recovery.[cxxi]

This inevitably takes the pressure off institutions by enabling them to share the weight of their mission with other entities. Cooperation is imperative among institutions in the fields of climate change adaptation and natural disaster mitigation. No organization has the capacity and the resources to prepare for and recover from natural disasters.

It takes a village.

For churches, cooperation starts with white faith leaders connecting with, learning from, and following the lead of black faith leaders. White churches can form loose networks with black and brown churches to be exposed to external view points and strategies to mitigate the disruption in their communities.

Collaboration

Collaboration is the next step in the process by which institutions become interdependent and maximize resources, ideas, and personnel to mitigate disruption from natural disasters. Collaboration goes beyond cooperation's initial engagement for mutual beneficence. Collaboration is useful in assessing risk, building resilience, and implementing strategies that enable institutions to plan and prepare for natural disasters. Public-private partnerships are one of many collaborative approaches institutions can take to build resilience in their cities. Boin writes, "Public-private partnerships are those in which groups from the public sector ally with a private entity to develop and fund a project together."[cxxii]

There are practical ways to prepare for civil unrest. Nancy Rogers argues that leaders can make a difference by joining with other groups to mitigate the harmful effects of sociopolitical unrest. She writes, "Mediation-wise attorneys can play an effective role in preparing for—and perhaps forestalling violence connected with—community unrest, as well as strengthening their public leaders' abilities to deal with people's concerns and building trust among communities within the community."cxxiii

Similar to mediation-wise attorneys, pastors and faith leaders have a unique opportunity to prepare for civil unrest before it occurs. This can be done through a variety of ways. One way is to collaborate with existing community stakeholders to bring to light the concerns and issues that contribute to racialized storms. Rogers writes that "mediation-wise attorneys can convene representatives of the broader community to develop the antidote to violence and costly destruction by addressing deep community concerns and preparing leaders to act wisely in the early hours and days of civil unrest when it occurs."cxxiv She claims that community leaders desire collaboration with other institutions and are open to new ideas for building resiliency in their respective communities.

Coordination

The U.S. Department of Justice's Community Relations Service provides a model that churches can follow to collaborate with communities during times of racial distress.

> The Community Relations Service (CRS), a component of the U.S. Department of Justice, is the federal government's "peacemaker" for community conflicts and tensions arising from difference of race, color, and national origin. CRS was created by the Civil Rights Act of 1964 and is the only federal component dedicated to assist state and local units of government, private and public organizations, and community groups with preventing and resolving racial and ethnic tensions, conflicts, and civil disorders, with the intent of restoring

racial stability and harmony...CRS conciliators work with state and local officials and community leaders to provide a wide variety of services to address racial issues and prevent violence. CRS' services include contributing expertise and guidance on methods and policies that calm racial tensions and conflicts. Enhancing strategies of state and local governments and community groups to prevent and respond to civil disorders. Improving lines of communication between parties experiencing racial tension or conflict, including federal, state, and local governments and community leaders and residents. Helping schools and universities effectively deal with incidents of racial tensions or violence.[cxxv]

Rogers highlights Sanford as an example of a city that successfully utilized the CRS to mitigate racial tension and implement change in police practices.

Coincidentally, some months before the shooting, the city of Sanford had employed—for duties independent of potential unrest—Andrew Thomas, a mediator with decades of experience dealing with community conflict in New York. After the shooting, Thomas coordinated with CRS and helped local officials arrange police protocols, develop communications strategies, create stakeholder groups that spanned community divisions, and convene long-term discussions that resulted in changes in law enforcement practices. Though demonstrations sometimes swelled to represent more than 60% of Sanford's population, the protests were peaceful, and police did not arrest any demonstrators. Perhaps most important, Thomas continues to facilitate talks that have already led to broadly embraced changes.[cxxvi]

The events in Sanford following the shooting pose a powerful example of coordination, "the combination of parts to achieve most effective or harmonious results."[cxxvii] Coordination results in improved communication because, as different entities work in concord, they must share and disseminate information.[cxxviii] Coordination challenges the silo mentality that plagues organizations. It's far easier to maintain systems and processes that work within an institution. However, communication can become complex when you're dealing with a number of different institutions that have different ethos, policies, and processes. Despite the complexity, coordination, in the long run, is better for an organization in the field of natural disaster mitigation.

Pastors across a city could coordinate their communication by conducting a city-wide sermon series on racial reconciliation and healing. Before a racialized crisis strikes, they could implement a plan to share notes and speak on racial tension the Sunday after the issue has hit. Imagine if several dozen pastors preached the same sermon (tailored and adapted to their congregations but essentially the same message) amid racial division and tension.

Cooperation, collaboration, and coordination are all aimed at fostering unity, a major point Jesus prayed for in his disciples: "May they experience such perfect unity that the world will know that you sent me and that you love them as much as you love me."[cxxix] Imagine, in a demonstration of unity, if congregations joined with other congregations and rented out a spacious venue in their city to conduct a worship service that would allow for individual and communal lament; a service where people from all colors and backgrounds could pray together and worship together under one roof. Imagine if churches collaborated to host a city-wide forum that brought awareness to the underlying factors that cause massive amounts of unrest when racialized storms strike. The possibilities are endless.

Preparing for a Racial Crisis

Below is a seven-step process that can help a church become ready for the disruption from a racialized crisis.

Organize

The first step in this process is to "gather together a core team of stakeholders who are likely to have the most capacity, whether in time, interest, ability, resources, or networks."[cxxx] Church leaders can implement this step by working to recruit people within their congregations that have a desire for racial justice, healing, and equity. Holding an interest meeting about the subject of race relations is an approach a church leader could take to generate attention toward the subject.

The point of an informational meeting is to provide an overview of the project to potential team members, to discuss roles and responsibilities of team members, and to determine whether others should be actively recruited to join an advisory group or taskforce to provide ongoing feedback to the core team."[cxxxi] The goal is to develop a core team that will "contribute to the design and execution of a broader community engagement strategy."[cxxxii] This team essentially becomes an engine of ideation in the congregation.

Kaplan and Donovan write about establishing infrastructure that will support lasting change within an organization. They propose creating a diversity council, which they claim is "a very effective tool for creating a strategy and jump-starting or overseeing implementation."[cxxxiii] They define a diversity council's "primary role is to act as a bridge between business case for action and the strategy for implementation."[cxxxiv] Additional roles of the diversity council include strategy development, change management, and communication.[cxxxv]

Connect

The second step is to engage in cooperation, collaboration, and eventually coordination with outside members in the community. Once a team of stakeholders within the congregation is established and has clarified goals and the purpose of engagement, that team should begin to look for outside groups that could meaningfully contribute to the mission of building resilience to racialized storms in the outside community. Cooperating and collaborating with outside groups gives a congregation the chance to maximize the impact of its strategies and affect a group of neighborhoods and possibly an entire city. "Creating partnerships at this stage ensures adequate attention to different analytical perspectives from various stakeholders."[cxxxvi] Working with outside groups gives a congregation the ability to amplify its resources and influence.

Assess

It is vital to recognize how important it is to accumulate and synthesize information on a congregation's potential vulnerability. Collecting and synthesizing information about an organization or community's vulnerability is key to fully grasping the reality that organization lives in. This information helps to improve processes, systems, and individuals within an organization. This improvement enables an institution to be more effective in achieving its mission. Clarifying the congregation's attitudes and beliefs is vital to know where to begin in building resilience to racialized storms. If the topography of a city shows that a certain part of a community lies in a floodplain and is thus susceptible to floods, then city planners and residents can act to mitigate potential damage in the case of a hurricane or torrential downpour.

However, one must know the contours of one's community to effectively plan and prevent devastation. Evaluating the vulnerability (whether it be having a significant percentage of people with racially prejudiced attitudes or a sizable percentage of people that believe inaccurate racial stereotypes) of a congregation is tantamount to a sustainable strategy. Lovett Weems writes that, "dependable data are needed in an accessible format...The opinions, perceptions, and ideas people have about the congregation are equally important. Such feedback regarding the current situation and future needs of the church's ministries is essential in visioning."[cxxxvii] Pastors need to create feedback loops to determine where their congregations stand on issues.

Envision

Lovett Weems explains the concept of vision as "a picture of a preferred future."[cxxxviii] He goes on to quote Rueben P. Job:

> Vision is a gift from God. It is the reward of disciplined,
> faithful, and patient listening to God. Vision allows us
> to see beyond the barriers and obstacles to our mission.
> Vision catches us up, captivates and compels us to act.
> Vision is the gift of eyes of faith to see the invisible, to
> know the unknowable, to think the unthinkable, to
> experience the not yet. Vision allows us to see signs of
> the kingdom now in our midst. Vision gives us focus,
> energy, the willingness to risk. It is our vision that
> draws us forward.[cxxxix]

Weems quotes Aristotle, who says that "the soul never thinks
without a picture."[cxl] People are not going to move unless
they have a picture of what's possible. It is vital that church
leaders, as they journey on the process of effective
responsiveness to racial crises, give a clear picture of what
direction they are going in and the potential benefits that
direction will yield. The step of envisioning isn't about
generating an arbitrary plan. It requires articulating a
picture of where that organization could be and articulating
that picture in a way that is compelling so that others will
take up the mantle and run with the vision. The process of
envisioning should be undertaken with the group of
stakeholders after a proper assessment of the congregation's
attitudes on racial issues has been completed.

Prioritize

During the prioritizing phase, the core group begins to list
and rank the list of options and strategies that have been
generated during the envision step. "The preparation phase
is where goals are set and the leaders of the group can clarify

the desired outcomes and the benchmarks that will indicate progress along the way. This is where policies, procedures, and processes are developed to drive diversity and racial reconciliation change initiatives into the institutional culture."[cxli] The core group that has been organized must take time to pray and discern which strategies from the vision are undertaken first.

Implement

Once strategies are prioritized, churches need to start working toward their goals. The implementation phase is an exciting time as churches embark on the journey of resiliency. The implementation phase "requires groups to define who will do what, and when, with regard to the execution of disaster management plans...it is time to identify manageable tasks and responsible parties. At this stage planners can help participants break strategies down into manageable tasks, effectively converting vision into action."[cxlii] The core group team should not have to execute all the tasks.

Monitor and Evaluate

The final step in the process is to implement measures that allow a church to effectively monitor and evaluate its progress in the implementation phases. Whether an elder's board or the taskforce itself, a strategy is needed to ensure accountability and efficiency in the process.

PART THREE

RESPONSIVENESS

The third segment of the Racial Crisis Framework is Responsiveness. This section emphasizes the need for a timely and dynamic response when a racialized crises occurs and produces profound racial division and tension. The Responsiveness section highlights the role of the prophet in ancient Israel as a model to respond in time of national distress. Contemporary Christian leaders cannot remain silent when these crises occur. In addition to the lack of knowledge regarding the lived experience of black people, the proclivity to silence is often the result of not wanting to "rock the boat," or offend anyone.

However, Christian leaders must understand that they make matters worse by not responding in times of crisis. Responding during times of national crisis is part of the job as a leader. Comforting God's people is part of the role of being a shepherd. The silence of white Christian leaders is deafening and painful to people of color. Jim Wallis recalled a conference call he had with several faith leaders.

> On that call, the leader of a nationwide network of black clergy, said even more painful to many black pastors than America's continuing racism is "the silence of white Christians." Black pastors still don't hear very many of their white clergy brothers and sisters in Christ speaking with prophetic clarity about the stark differences in the ways that white and black young men, even in their respective congregations, continue to be treated by police officers. And why the silence, when almost none of the officers involved in the shootings of young African American have yet to be held accountable?[cxliii]

Later in the article, Wallis remarks how Martin Luther King, Jr. greatly admired Bonhoeffer and subsequently goes on to quote Bonhoeffer's famous line on silence. "Silence in the face of evil is itself evil. God will not hold us guiltless. Not to speak is to speak. Not to act is to act."[cxliv] Chilling words, but painstakingly true. Religious leaders who do not speak out in times of great racial discord and tension are communicating a great deal about where they are, what they think, and where their congregation is on the issue of racism.

This section of the framework directly impacts people in a congregation, community, and city. Faith leaders who break the silence and speak out will face backlash. King suffered a severe backlash from President Lyndon B. Johnson's administration when he began to speak out against the Vietnam war in the late 1960s. Jesus's teaching on counting the cost is a crucial lesson for pastors to learn.

You have to understand that there is a cost associated with speaking out about racism.

There is a strong chance that church leaders will offend racist whites, or whites who simply desire not to bring "politics" into the pulpit when they speak out about the gross inequities and disparities that we see in America today. That is why the role of the prophet is the focus on this section of the book. The prophet was God's spokesman and communicated God's words with clarity and conviction. Contemporary Christian leaders can learn a great deal about how prophets communicated in times of crisis and apply the characteristics of this critical leadership function to their own congregation.

VI

Insights from the Prophetic Tradition

I do not do so from a standpoint of arrogance, of being above the fray, pointing the finger without an awareness of my own frailty, my own suffering and need for salvation. And yet I must nevertheless prophesy, not because I'm perfect, but because I'm called.

—MICHAEL ERIC DYSON, *TEARS WE CANNOT STOP*

Arrival, a thrilling cinematic treasure, graced theaters across the country on November 11, 2016. The film is introspective and philosophical. Its existential overtones are felt throughout its hour-and-fifty-eight-minute duration. The mysterious science fiction movie chronicles the story of twelve extraterrestrial spacecraft that touch down across Earth. The aliens "arrive," but do not appear to be belligerent. Their ships leave no environmental footprint while maintaining a stationary position where they touched down. The million-dollar question everyone in the world is asking is, "Why are they here? What is their purpose?" Amy Adams plays the brilliant but melancholy linguist, Dr. Louise Banks. Banks is recruited by the U.S. government to decipher the strange alien language and to decipher their intent on Earth. Her co-star, Jeremy Renner, plays a quirky astrophysicist, Ian Donnelly, who helps analyze the language of the alien species.

The movie effectively highlights the importance of linguistics; how the words we speak and write have the potential to make an enormous impact on the world around us. The quote is noteworthy: communication can be used to build or tear down. Indeed, dozens of biblical scriptures bring attention to the power of words. The book of Proverbs is notable for its many verses on the impact of words. Proverbs 15:1 is a classic example: "A gentle answer deflects anger, but harsh words make temper flare." Proverbs 16:24 states, "Kind words are like honey—sweet to the soul and healthy for the body." Finally, Proverbs 18:21 gives readers a sobering perspective on the effect of words: "The tongue can bring death or life; those who love to talk will reap the consequences."

Language can also be misconstrued and thus lead to conflict. In the film, Dr. Banks and her colleague, Ian, make considerable progress in decrypting the complex language of the Heptapods (extraterrestrial race). As their vocabulary grows, the characters discover a very important message the Heptapods are trying to communicate to humanity, "Offer weapon." All hell breaks loose after they translate the message in English and believe it to be a credible threat. The governments across the world, already on edge because of the lack of communication on the alien's intent, ready themselves for war. Dr. Banks is convinced that the translation means more than the concept of a weapon and could have double meaning such as "device, apparatus, or way."

As Louise immerses herself in the Heptapods' language structure, she begins to experience time in a nonlinear way. She finds herself experiencing events not only in real time, but in the past and future. Nonlinear time is essentially being able to "view the past, present, and future simultaneously."[cxlv] The Heptapods inform Louise that their intent on Earth is to share their language which also includes their unique perception of time. Except for past people groups like the Mayans, humans traditionally think of time progressing in a linear fashion. We eventually learn that the Heptapods' purpose on Earth is to offer a "weapon/tool" to help unify humanity, not destroy it.

What does this have to do with developing a framework that enables faith leaders and churches to properly prepare for and respond to racially charged events that cause upheaval and division in the sociopolitical landscape of our communities and cities? Everything, because language

matters. What we say and how we say it matters. A robust
and substantive response to tragedy matters. When a
racialized storm strikes, what will a pastor say the following
Sunday morning? If a thousand neo-Nazis march in your
city, what words will the pastors utter to their
congregations?

The Necessity of Responsiveness

Responsiveness to racialized crises is critical to the
credibility of the American church. People of color are
heartbroken when these situations arise. If diversity is truly
an important goal in the American church, a strong and
forceful response is crucial. Waiting for the crisis to subside
is simply unacceptable. Unfortunately, many white Christian
leaders resist the impulse to say something in fear that they
are placating to the news media's exaggeration of racialized
tragedies. Some of this comes from a deep distrust of what
President Trump calls, "Fake News." They believe that
they'll be more informed if they wait until the anger and
pain subsides. That is not a wise strategy.

Kevin Clay chronicles his experiences with his white
pastor, who chose to remain silent after the deaths of
Michael Brown and John Crawford. He writes with a
perspective that many black members who attend majority-
white congregations share:

> Ignoring the deaths of Michael Brown, John Crawford,
> Jordan Davis and others in service of placating white
> congregants is just as dangerous and problematic as
> overtly racist responses. Silence inadvertently
> communicates to the white members that these aren't

important matters or that they are not relevant to the faith. The Sundays after the Brown shooting and the release of the video showing Crawford being gunned down in Walmart, my pastor was noticeably silent on both incidents and ambiguously generic in his message. What did come across felt like an empty attempt to satisfy his own conscience by simply acknowledging that there is "division" in the country, without naming the divided parties or directing the church to support any stakeholders. As a black member of a majority-white congregation after the Brown and Crawford incidents, I find it alienating when a pastor ignores these issues or halfheartedly speaks about "diversity."[cxlvi]

Silence is simply not an option in a sociopolitical climate that has grown increasingly, partisan, divisive, and hostile. Race in America has been and will always be a divisive subject. Racism has been woven into the very fabric of America. From its very inception, policies, laws, and decisions have been made to oppress black and brown people. Simply remaining silent, in hopes of not being divisive, is imprudent.

Father Bryan Massingale, writing from the perspective of a priest in the Catholic church, implores pastors to denounce racism as a sin from the pulpit.

> For too many Catholic Christians, their racism and that of their friends, neighbors, and family members is abetted by the silence of their pastors and teachers. A permissive silence. A silence that gives comfort to those who harbor resentment, fear, and even hatred in their hearts. A silence that allows Jesus and racial animosity to coexist in their souls. Such silence allows a young man like Roof to draw a picture of Jesus in a hate-filled

journal. He probably never heard anyone tell him this very simple truth: "You cannot be a racist and a Christian at the same time." The silence of the church's leadership in the face of continuing injustice is the faith community's deepest act of complicity in American racism.cxlvii

Massingale challenges the narrative that many white Christians repeat when confronted with matters of systemic racism, that the Dylann Roofs of the world are mere aberrations and thus do not warrant a response or holistic strategy to root out racism in their congregations. His indictment of a "silence that allows Jesus and racial animosity to coexist" in the innermost recesses of their souls is significant.

The white American church constructed a theology of segregation and inferiority. This is evident most notably in several major denominational splits leading up to the American Civil War. This theology, now largely discredited today, still runs through the veins of contemporary Christians. Sean Watkins describes how silence about racial tension and division is theologically irresponsible and wrong because of the example that Christ gives us in the scriptural narrative. Speaking on the Charleston shooting, he writes:

> Whether your congregation has responded to the racial tensions in the country previously or not—that does not matter now. As Aslan said to Lucy in PRINCE CASPIAN, "I cannot tell you what would have happened; I can only tell you what will." The time is before you now to pastor congregations prophetically like never before. Racism has not only been in the country, it has now—again—reared its ugly head in the church. When Jesus encountered an evil spirit in the Synagogue in Mark 1,

He was not silent. He did not ignore it. He addressed it publicly and removed it from His presence...Whether it is the topic, a point, a sub-point, or a prayer request in your congregation, I urge you to say something. I submit all of our churches are in different places and different degrees of response are warranted. But no response is unacceptable.[cxlviii]

Responding to racial tragedies is not just socially responsible, but theologically warranted. Church leaders typically are reluctant to speak on these matters for fear that politics should be left out of the pulpit. Unfortunately, politics and policies affect the well-being of millions in America. I often believe this sentiment is heavily influenced by the hyper-partisanship of today. The reality is, politics are simply the public negotiation and allocation of what we value. To be silent in hopes of not wading into contentious politics exposes the privilege that many pastors (and their congregations) possess.

Tim Scott (R), U.S. senator for the state of South Carolina, stated that President Trump's untimely response to the events in Charlottesville was damaging to his presidency and the country. Scott highlighted the fact that Trump's response was weak and late: "I hope this serves as a lesson for all that when a community grieves, when Americans look for guidance after such a crushing and devastating attack like the one that unraveled this weekend in Charlottesville, we must take a firm stance against hate and violence," he wrote in a statement.[cxlix] In the wake of President Trump's sluggish and tepid response to Charlottesville, nine CEOs that comprised the president's business and manufacturing advisory council indicated that they would no longer serve on the council and immediately stepped down. Whether it's in their communities or a major news story that grabs headlines across the nation, faith leaders need to speak up.

The Prophet

In biblical times, prophets led, spoke, and comforted Israel in times of national crisis. During periods characterized by uncertainty, prophets boldly spoke on behalf God and challenged the prevailing mindset of the day. Learning from the prophets can help pastors offer a robust and substantive response to racialized tragedies. Gene Tucker notes how important the role of the prophet is for our contemporary society:

> I am convinced that we must take seriously a prophetic role for the church in our society. Woe to us—and our nation and our world—if we do not. The model for that role, to some extent at least, must be found in the Old Testament prophets. They cannot, of course, have the last word; that must be found in the Gospel. But even Jesus had a prophetic role and called his disciples to be, among other things, prophetic.[cl]

John Goldingay in writes that defining prophets can be complex because of the many personalities that occupied the office. These men and women spoke out on a variety of different subjects.

> They can be seen as social critics (Amos), political critics (Isaiah), moral critics (Jeremiah), and religious critics (Ezekiel)...A prophet shares God's nightmares and dreams, speaks like a poet and behaves like an actor, is

> not afraid to be offensive, confronts the confident with
> rebuke and downcast with hope, mostly speaks to the
> people of God, is independent of the institutional
> pressures of church and state, is a scary person
> mediating the activity of a scary God, intercedes with
> boldness and praises with freedom, ministers in a way
> that reflects his or her personality and time.[cli]

The prophet was God's messenger who would pronounce oracles of God's judgment or salvation depending on the time and context.

Traits from Prophetic Leadership

Prophets were called by God and continuously advocated on matters that concerned God and the marginalized in Hebraic society. What we need now more than ever is prophetic leadership from white pastors. The following section in this chapter consist of traits from the Hebraic prophets that we need in our contemporary times.

Truth Telling from Moral Clarity

Prophetic leadership necessitates a moral decisiveness that is both specific and courageous. It must be a conviction derived from God alone. If we do not call the society to account in the name of God, who will? If we do not hold out a vision of a just and righteous society, who will? If we see disaster coming, we should have the courage to say so because we know that, as Peter said to the high priest, we must obey God rather than men.

American culture has become increasingly therapeutic.

great risk in their professions as communicators on God's behalf. When racialized crises occur, church leaders must be faithful to tell the truth about America's history of racial injustice, present-day structural racism, and why their black brothers and sisters are hurting. This is not an easy task because of the strong sense of exceptionalism that runs through the vein of American culture. Walter Brueggemann comments on the pervasive influence of American exceptionalism:

> Thus we have complete confidence in the American way of life that is much confused with the promises of the Gospel. Across the entire political spectrum, we imagine our way in the world is the right way and are largely incapable of noticing the trouble and suffering evoked in the world by U.S. practices and policies. More than that, we try not to take with seriousness the unraveling of the human fabric in our society because of greed that very often eventuates in violence, even if covert violence.[cliii]

What often prevents truth-telling in America is the consumption of distorted truth about this nation's record on race and human rights. Space will not allow for an extensive survey of the origins and present-day ramifications of the ideology of American exceptionalism. However, it should be noted that this ideology is largely responsible for silence that befalls numerous pastors on the Sunday morning following a racialized tragedy in America. It is also why white Christians look at black ministers cross-eyed when they hear these ministers criticizing America's historical record. President Barack Obama's former pastor, Jeremiah Wright, is a great example. White Christians across America were

120

clutching their pearls when they heard excerpts from his sermons including the infamous line, "God Bless, America? No, God Damn, America." Never mind the fact that this man served his country as member of the United States Marine Corps. His criticism of American exceptionalism sent many white Christians into a tail spin.

Grounded in Social Awareness

Social awareness is another trait church leaders can learn from as they endeavor to offer a robust response to racialized crises. The traditional view of prophets as wild vagabonds with radical messages misses the point that these men and women were intricately connected to their community. Tucker notes the prophet's communal connectivity:

> The prophets were deeply involved in the political, social, and religious affairs of their nation. They addressed not only groups and congregations, but specific individuals—often by name—including kings and princes, and even the nation as a whole...Moreover, they continue to judge us for our silence in the face of any and all forms of injustice and oppression. It is difficult to place the newspaper and the prophetic books side by side and look away with an easy conscience.[cliv]

When it comes to the church, there is a propensity to want to focus on the needs and affairs within the congregation; to withdraw from the world and maintain an insular way of living and thinking. Michael Emerson and Christian Smith write in *Divided by Faith* that American religion is organized in a way that produces churches that are consumed with belonging, harmony, and security for the congregation.[clv] We can often retreat to our bubbles and form echo chambers where we're surrounded with people that look, think, and act like us. But are we attentive to a suffering world or are we enraptured with, as Soong-Chan Rah states, "success-centered triumphalism?" The prophet challenges us to be bound to our congregation and our wider community.

Practically, faith leaders can utilize the three C's (cooperation, collaboration, and coordination) discussed in Chapter 5, but instead of working solely with churches, they can begin to build networks and partnerships with nonprofits and city entities that are outside of their immediate network. During my time in graduate school at Texas A&M University, I took part in a summer internship at the Jacksonville mayor's office. At the time, Jacksonville, Florida, was plagued with violent crime. At one point, the city had so many homicides that it replaced Miami as the murder capital of Florida. The mayor's office, with close coordination with the city council and Jacksonville sheriff's department, came up with a comprehensive criminal justice policy to curb the violence.

The internship afforded me the opportunity to travel with the mayor to town hall meetings to sell his policy to the public. Traveling to the north side of the city (where much of the crime was occurring) forced me to confront a different community ethos from what I had been accustomed to living on the south side of the city. The new social awareness informed my attitudes and beliefs about traditionally disinvested communities. Sitting for hours in those town halls, listening to hundreds of fearful and concerned residents talk about the need for the city to do something urgent was life-changing. Pastors would be wise to attend local town hall meetings put on by elected officials, city council meetings, and any event that has a focus on race and justice. This intentionality will enable pastors to be more grounded in the entirety of their community. Becoming more socially aware is especially important in an American culture that stresses radical individualism, often at the expense of community.

A Word of God Movement

The prophet was driven to point the Israelites to God's chosen path through the scriptural narrative. Church leaders' response to racialized crises must be driven by the scriptural narrative. Prophetic leadership necessitates incorporating what God says in His Word. Pastors should fight against the tendency to overly rely on sociological analysis, American civil religion, or secular liberalism.

One of the best-known examples of a prophetic leader utilizing this trait is the late Martin Luther King, Jr. Richard Lischer writes extensively on King's life, leadership, and ministry in his book *The Preacher King.* He makes the case in his book, that King's leadership during Civil Rights movement in America often utilized scripture. Lischer notes that "Under [King's] leadership, the quest for equality and justice became a Word of God Movement."[clvi] For King, prophetic leadership was to bear the mantle of the Word—to utter, in the vein of Moses or Isaiah, "Thus says the Lord."[clvii]

King was adamant that the Civil Rights Movement was a Word of God Movement. Richard Lischer, describing King's philosophy of the Bible, states that King "believed that the preached Word performs a sustaining function for all who are oppressed, and the corrective function for all who know the truth but lead disordered lives. He believed that the Word of God possessed the power to change hearts of stone."[clviii] The theological disposition of the church demands that the body of Christ engage robustly in matters that produce social vulnerability. There are well over 2,000 verses in the Bible that deal with poverty and justice. Scripture is clear that God stands on the side of the oppressed.

King reminds contemporary faith leaders that Scripture is the basis for moral authority. The Civil Rights Movement was a Word of God Movement and King narrated the word by projecting those who marched, sat, and protested into the Scriptural narrative. He drew parallels to the Israelites exodus of Egypt and march to the promise land and African Americans marching to their promised freedoms enshrined in the Declaration of Independence and Constitution. The task is the same for contemporary Christian leaders.

The scriptural narrative transcended the discord and disunity of his day and inspired people to change, to overcome, and to revolt against the status quo. What America needs now more than ever is for faith leaders to stop hiding behind the stained-glass windows and dare to wade into the turbulent waters of culture armed with the sword of the Spirit. America needs church leaders to rise up and speak prophetically over the people of God in the nation. Will Willimon writes,

> Christian preaching begins, not with astute sociological analysis of the human condition, but rather with scripture. The biblical preacher, in service to the congregation, goes to the biblical text hoping to make a discovery. Then the preacher shares that discovery with

the congregation, taking that congregation on much of
the same journey as that preacher made in prayerful
confrontation with the text.[clix]

America needs new Martin Luther Kings who dare to use the
Word of God to speak out against racial, economic, and
societal ills of our day; to communicate with substance and
civility on the problems that American culture faces.
America needs new Martin Luther Kings who can transcend
racial divides, who can wield the Sword of the Spirit to cut
down the entrenched injustices and nihilism that
characterize today's society. America needs new leaders who
mobilize congregations to march around the walls of injustice
and shout that they would come down. Faith leaders must
understand how to apply God's word, specifically in the
context of racialized storms. The Word of God must be
utilized in the response that pastors give to comfort and
challenge their people.

Imagination

A survey of the great collections of Jeremiah, Isaiah, and
Ezekiel elucidate a pattern of prophets speaking in the
language of hope as the communities reside in a reality of
desolation. The prophets were situated in the exilic period of
the Jewish community. God's people had been scattered
because of their unfaithfulness to Yahweh. Their world had
crumbled and it had seemed that God had abandoned them
forever. The prophets, amidst the exile, were consistent in
their message of hope to the Hebrew children that their
mourning would not last forever.

Walter Brueggemann describes the power of an imaginative picture given from God that the prophets of old possessed and utilized as a tool to speak of redemption and restoration when the people of Israel could not:

> The task of prophetic ministry is to nurture, nourish, and evoke a consciousness and perception alternative to the consciousness and perception of the dominant culture around us...That alternative consciousness to be nurtured, on the one hand, serves to criticize in dismantling the dominant consciousness...On the other hand, that alternative consciousness to be nurtured serves to energize persons and communities by its promise of another time and situation toward which the community of faith may move. To that extent it attempts to do what the conservative tendency has done, to live in fervent anticipation of the newness that God has promised and will surely give.[clx]

The prophets implanted an idea fundamentally different from what had been happening to the Hebrew exiles. The dominant thinking was characterized by a sense of abandonment, rejection, and confusion. In that context, the prophetic word—filled with faith that Israel is still Yahweh's possession—promised hope and a better day. Even when the individual or community fails in its faithfulness to God, "hope is possible because the future does not depend on human efforts alone, but the future is under God's sovereign rule."

Racialized crises produce similar sentiments that the people of Israel experienced. While Americans don't have to worry about exile or living under an oppressive foreign regime, there is a sense of emotional abandonment, rejection, and fear that can often afflict individuals and communities.

Church leaders must articulate the hope that Christians have in a God who time and time again has rescued and provided for them.

Contemporary Christian leaders engage in imaginative work during a racialized crises when they remind their congregations of the reality of another realm, a heavenly reality that is that exhibits an otherworldly love. The prophetic tradition challenges us to remember who we are—a people that are loved by this transcendent, omniscient, and omnipotent God. This takes innovation, imagination, and energy. What made Martin Luther King, Jr. special was the imaginative picture he possessed of a better America. He had a dream of an America that was fundamentally true to what it said it would be in the Declaration of Independence and Constitution.

Lament

Prophets in ancient Israel frequently used the function of lament to process pain. Soong-Chan Rah claims that lament is missing as an essential component of the Christian faith. This missing element makes it especially difficult to respond in times of tragedy because the American Christian church has embraced a theology of celebration and triumphalism. When faced with the communal suffering and pain that blacks feel from racialized crises, the American Christian church can often find itself ill-equipped in its response to these storms. Rah states, "A triumphant and success-oriented narrative limits the twenty-first-century American evangelical theological imagination. The narrative of triumph silences a narrative of suffering."[clxi]

To conclude this section, I offer a sermon and a blog as written pieces that illustrate what it might look like to preach on the subject of racial division. The purpose behind these works was to give hope in the midst of despair. My objective was to help individuals navigate through the intense sociocultural disruption that was being generated from racialized storms.

The first piece, "From the Fatigue of Despair to the Buoyancy of Hope," was a sermon I gave in response to the horrific tragedy at Emmanuel AME Church in Charleston, South Carolina. I was accepted into the DMin program at Duke a month before and, in a way, this tragedy set the stage for what I wanted to write about in my doctoral thesis. I was distraught after the shooting. I remember pacing, praying, and reflecting in my kitchen two days after the massacre. I was glued to CNN and increasingly getting more and more agitated. I wanted to do something. I wanted to say something, but didn't know where to begin.

Unanticipatedly, an idea came. I realized, in the spur of the moment, that I needed to be in Charleston. Sure, it was a bit rash, but I felt the need to be on the streets, with the people, to get a sense of what was going on in the city. At the time, news crews from all over the world had descended upon Charleston to capture the story. I told my wife that I felt that I should go to Charleston. Her response was vintage Tracy: "What in the world are you going to do there?" I admittedly had no clue what to do, but I had a strong inclination that I needed to be there. I found a hotel thirty minutes outside of Charleston (all the hotels in the area were booked at that point), called three friends to come with me, gassed up the car, and left for Charleston only a couple of hours after the idea first came to me.

Being on the streets of Charleston was a rush. It was a hot June day and tens of thousands of people were milling around downtown. News crews were covering the scene live. Jesse Jackson walked right past me on his way to an interview with CNN. President Obama was in town at the time delivering the eulogy of the nine souls who had perished. I started going up to random people and asking if they were from Charleston and why the city was not erupting with anger. Ferguson was still fresh on everyone's mind and Dylann Roof explicitly stated he desired to start a race war with his actions. The streets of Charleston were largely peaceful. I spoked to dozens of people and several them said that it was the forgiveness of the families that ultimately saved the city. Instead of erupting in rage, the families provided solace to a city on edge, but publicly forgiving Roof.

Eventually, I grew tired from walking around and did something I probably wasn't supposed to do. I snuck around security and walked right into Mother Emmanuel AME Church. I walked around for a little while, took some pictures, and finally sat in the sanctuary. I was overwhelmed by the peace of God in that church. Charleston changed me. I went back home two days later. I decided to tell my group about my experience and preach about racism at our Young Professional's worship service. This sermon not only reflects that worship service, but what I experienced on the streets of Charleston.

The final piece, entitled "My Heart Breaks for Baton Rouge," was written during the racialized storms during the summer of 2016. Alton Sterling was shot and killed by police in an altercation in Baton Rouge, Louisiana. This tragedy was personal to me. I worked as a project manager, specializing in neighborhood revitalization and economic development in Baton Rouge. The neighborhood where Alton Sterling was shot and killed in was one of the areas my agency focused its revitalization efforts. I worked in that community and knew residents there. Baton Rouge is a city I have great affection for and once called home. It was devastating to see the city I loved go through such a traumatic event.

A day later, Philando Castile was gunned down in front of his girlfriend and her four-year-old daughter. I found out at church a couple of days later that one of his family members was friend of my wife and I. Talking to his family member made his death and the subsequent unrest deeply unsettling. The blog piece I wrote was intended to help my friends and congregants navigate through the emotions of this tragedy. I desired to help them know what to pray for during that time of national crisis. It was during this time that I began to draw parallels between climate change and natural disaster and the sociopolitical unrest that is produced from these racialized tragedies. My prayer is that these pieces inspire faith leaders to stand up and boldly speak out against injustice and communicate the hope that is in our Lord Jesus Christ.

Fatigue of Despair to the Buoyancy of Hope: A Sermon in Response to the Tragedy in at Emmanuel AME

Tonight, I'm interrupting our series to talk about what happened last week in Charleston, South Carolina, at Emmanuel AME Church. We cannot respond to every tragedy in the news—the news is a 24/7 cycle of negativity. It's hard to watch and respond to the news. It just seems like so many horrible things are happening in our country and around the world. If you're not careful, you can find yourself getting numb to the pain and tragedy. My daddy was a news anchor. I certainly wasn't numb to what happened in Charleston last week.

Like many of you, when I heard the news of the shooting at Emmanuel AME Church in Charleston, South Carolina, I was heartbroken. Nine sweet souls perished in a Bible study at the hands of an evil and hateful human being. I was glued to my iPad and iPhone, constantly checking updates and seeing what pastors, politicians, and businessman were saying about the events. This event was very significant to me personally as an African American and as a pastor.

It blew my mind that the sweet parishioners of Emmanuel AME welcomed and accepted Dylann Roof and he returned that gift of hospitality and acceptance with violence, malice, and murder. The shooter was methodical with his research. He knew what he wanted to accomplish when he walked inside that church. He said that he hoped to start a race war from his actions. Praise be to God that the Lord has used his hateful action to reignite a much-needed dialogue about the reality of race relations in America.

The shooting at Emmanuel AME was horrific, evil, and
hateful. We must pray for victim's families. This tragedy has
once again elevated the topic of race relations to the forefront
of our national attention. During the last couple of years, our
nation has experienced a series of tragic events that have
aggravated the wound of racism in our country. There has
been an inordinate amount of racially charged rhetoric, city-
wide rioting in major American cities, hundreds of thousands
of people marching, academic symposiums, speeches from
the president. What happened in Charleston matters. The
national discourse it has produced matters. It matters to us
right here in Jacksonville, Florida, because racism is alive
and well in this country, both interpersonally and
institutionally. I feel like a lot of Christians and generally
people across America treat racism like it's going extinct.
Unfortunately, it's not.

I'm not talking to you tonight as a government official.
Though I majored in political science and worked in
government for several years. I believe in the power of
judicial, executive, and legislative process. I'm not talking to
you as a doctoral student at Duke University whose thesis
will be on racial reconciliation. I'm talking to you as a pastor.
As a shepherd, to encourage you to take the lead on the issue
of racial prejudice. I want to encourage you to take the lead
in being a voice for inclusivity, dignity, and equality in the
face of rhetoric that is divisive and demeaning.

My desire is to equip you with the right perspective to
have concerning all of this. I want you to see the big picture.
There are no easy answers when it comes to racial division in
America. I think we want an easy answer. I think a lot of
people thought that Barack Obama's election to the

presidency would be the silver bullet that solved racial inequality and prejudice in our country. It's fascinating that during his presidency we've seen a level of rioting and unrest not seen in decades.

Charleston is more than aberration. This tragedy brings up a lot questions and issues, including greater gun control, confederate flag, inequality in our education system, violent racial history, poverty, crime.

We have come a long way as a country. I lived in Oxford, Mississippi, in the early '90s. The scars of the Battle of Ole Miss were still evident nearly thirty years later. In September 1962, James Meredith, an Air Force veteran, applied to Ole Miss. The governor at the time tried to defy the Supreme Court's decision to admit Meredith. This situation triggered a crisis between the state of Mississippi and the federal government. When Meredith arrived at Ole Miss he had to be protected by U.S. marshals who were put in place by the Kennedy administration. A mob of thousands descended on the campus to disrupt Meredith's enrollment at the university.

Two people died and dozens were injured in the ensuing chaos. The Kennedy administration was forced to send in an army of 31,000 troops. Oxford, Mississippi, essentially was under military occupation. Can you believe that? Can you imagine that? An entire army descended on a small southern town to force one black man to be a college student.

In what essentially amounted to a military occupation, federal marshals were forced to remain with James Meredith for the entirety of his time at Ole Miss. Thirty years later, I ran around that campus as a wide-eyed eight-year-old boy with a daddy who was an adjunct professor at the university.

Twelve years after that, the student body elected Kim Dandridge as the first African American female student body president.

I want to encourage you to take the lead in healing the racial divide in our country. It's up to us as Christ followers to take the lead. Starbucks has tried to lead the charge, government officials are trying to lead the charge, comedians like Jon Stewart have tried to lead the charge, community activists like Al Sharpton and Jesse Jackson are trying to lead the charge, Hollywood is trying to lead the charge. The only way to lead and win on this issue is to diminish the kingdom of darkness by advancing the kingdom of God in the heart and minds of men and women. The kingdom of God must gain ground because as we come under God's dominion we are confronted with the racism and prejudice in our heart. Jesus and racism cannot coexist. We also must speak out about the structural inequalities that exist in America, particularly in our criminal justice system.

We cannot be silent or ignorant when it comes to this issue. My assignment is to equip you with the right perspective. I don't have a lot of time, but I will do my best because if you are not equipped on how to engage in the proper dialogue with this subject you'll be silent. And your silence can be deafening. It can be easy to stand by in passivity and acquiesce to racially charged language and jokes. We cannot be ignorant either, randomly spouting off our opinions without pausing to reflect, pray, or determine how best to build a bridge.

I remember being in high school and my scheduling got changed in the middle of the year so I couldn't have lunch with my friends who I normally sat with. I had one cross country teammate who sat with his group of friends from the IB program and so I started to sit with them. One guy in the group had a racist grandfather who would rail against black people. He would glowingly talk about how his grandfather would call black people Nigger. He would use the word Nigger to repeat verbatim what his grandpa said. The whole table would simultaneous cringe and laugh. Cringe, because there was a sixteen-year-old black kid (me) who was at the table, and laugh because they thought that racially insensitive language was funny.

I remember the pain, embarrassment, and shame whenever that kid would use racial epithets. Though, he didn't direct them specifically at me, the fact that he didn't care how I would receive them and the fact that none of the other students spoke up, was telling. The worse part about it is that I didn't say anything. I said nothing because I was embarrassed and I desperately wanted to be accepted. By not saying anything, my silence condoned what was happening and it continued to happen. Some of you have racist family members that love to joke around about racial matters. And although you may not agree with them your silence or participation in that joking condones that behavior. How many times, growing up, did Dylann Roof hear racist and offensive language about blacks before he started to truly believe it? How many people were around him and heard him spewing racist language, but chose not to say anything? Chose to be silent?

The shooting of those nine sweet souls in Charleston was a tragedy. And people just don't know what to do. The national media questions how this type of thing could happen in 2015. The *New York Times* claimed that "he touched the wrong nerve in a country struggling to confront racism and hatred in the days after nine black parishioners were killed during a Bible study in a South Carolina church." Why is it a struggle to confront racism and hatred? Because they do not have the right perspective. Because they adhere to a worldview called advancement thinking.

Advancement thinking is the idea that our cultural, political, and intellectual landscape will flourish through the inevitable progress of human reason and achievement. This worldview believes that as long as time progresses people will be more civil, or intelligent, and accepting. Unfortunately, it takes about thirty seconds of viewing CNN to see that worldview does not seem to be true. Despite our advancement, we still live in a world of war, famine, poverty, and disease. This advancement thinking seeps into our culture and can cloud and dilute the filter of the Gospel by thinking that human reason and achievement will ultimately drive progress. So the Charleston Church Massacre doesn't fit into the mold of inevitable progress and we wonder why horrific events like this happen?

This type of thinking is incorrect because it falsely assumes that if time passes mankind will progress. Advancement thinking does not consider what we, who ascribe to the Christian worldview, know so well, that is the power of sin that leads to a broken world. Humanity is fallen. It is in a state of total depravity. Corrupted. Decadent. Perverted. Deteriorating. This affects the individual heart and as it does the culture and society we live in. Racial prejudice is just one manifestation of the corruption of our souls.

We must realize our responsibility and take the

offensive. We cannot be reactionary or defensive. We must take the lead. The church leads on this issue and other societal ills through the proclamation of the Gospel and the advancement of the kingdom of God in the hearts and minds of men. It's when we see everything through the filter of Jesus.

It happens on a micro level, like a virus that sweeps through a physical body. The dominion and authority of Christ must break through the walls of sin in our soul. Before we can ever see macro-level change in a city, region, state, nation, we must look inwardly to see if our relationship with Jesus is transformational or if we simply adhering to institutional religion that lacks the power to change one's heart.

This is the Christ follower's ultimate weapon. While the congressman has legislation, the comedian has jokes, the president has executive authority, the Christ follower has the Gospel! I was so impacted by the shooting at Emmanuel AME that I drove up to Charleston two days after the shooting to get a sense of what was going on there. I felt God calling me to go to there to walk the streets and pray and love on people in the community. Three guys from our group joined me. Once we got there we spent several hours outside the church. There were literally thousands of people on the streets, holding signs, being interviewed by the news, and engaging in peaceful protest.

I was amazed at the peace, forgiveness, and love that was in Charleston. The sense of resilience in the people of Charleston was inspiring. I talked to several residents of the city and asked each of them the same set of questions. One of the questions I asked was: What is your explanation for the peace and unity that the city is experiencing right now? Person after person said that the forgiveness that was shown by the victim's families toward the shooter was one of the main reasons for the harmony that settled over the city.

I got the opportunity to go inside the church and sit down for half an hour. It was a bit surreal as I sat silently in a pew and prayed that God would wipe the tears from the people of Charleston's eyes. I prayed that His great love would penetrate hardened hearts and unleash a powerful resolve throughout the city; a resolve to not be overcome by hate, but instead be full of love. What the enemy meant for destruction and division, God turned it into healing and unity. I'm grateful for the opportunity to have witnessed such a powerful example of love.

Gospel change is about change of the heart. As you are reconciled with a just and holy God, that just and holy God calls you to reconcile with your fellow man. See at the end of the day it's a heart issue: "But the words you speak come from the heart—that's what defiles you. For from the heart come evil thoughts, murder, adultery, all sexual immorality, theft, lying, and slander."[clxii]

If we do not check our hearts. And if wrong perspectives, attitudes, thoughts that have not been touched by the transforming power of the Holy Spirit persist, they will be handed down to the next generation. The enemy of our soul is not just focused on your destruction, he is interested in handicapping the next generation with the sin you never received deliverance from...He desires for the next generation to be plagued with the same racism that this generation is plagued with.

SO HOW DO WE LEAD IN THIS TIME OF CRISIS?

By not standing by passively or silently when prejudicial words are uttered or jokes are made.

By praying fervently for our nation. Specifically, that racial wounds from the past would be heal. By listening emphatically. The Bible says that "spouting off before listening to the facts is both shameful and foolish. The tongue can bring death or life; those who love to talk will reap the consequences.[clxiii]

By making this ministry radically inclusive. Practicing exceptional hospitality to those who are ethnically and culturally different than you. Also, I think it's important to use and adopt inclusive language. Instead of they, them, those, it's we and us...

By following in Jesus's example of crossing cultural boundaries and connecting with people that are different than us.

By being a thermostat instead of a thermometer. When I walk into a room and I can tell that it is not a welcoming environment, I choose to turn up the temperature of acceptance and grace.

By advancing the Kingdom of God through the preaching of the Gospel.

I truly believe this type of leadership produces:

Acceptance of over rejection.

Trust over mistrust.

Love over hate.

Cognitive generosity over cognitive categorization.

Peace over anxiety.

Godly action over passivity.

Light over darkness.

Peace over hostility.

Kindness over malice.

Connection over division.

Inclusivity over exclusivity.

We lead by understanding the strategy of Satan which is to divide and conquer. Satan is real and he wants to steal trust, destroy relationships, and kill any chance of unity and harmony. But I thank God for his Word, because His Word reminds us that *the Son of God came to destroy the works of the devil.*clxiv

We must model our lives after Jesus. Jesus was cross-cultural. He broke down cultural barriers. He was a deity and yet became human and identified with our weaknesses. He walked several miles in our shoes. Philippians 2:7 says that, "Instead, he gave up his divine privileges; he took the humble position of a slave and was born as a human being." He was God, but crossed boundaries to become humans and identify with us to save us. Jesus cared about the people on the margins. He spent time with women, tax collectors, and the infirmed. He blessed children and spoke of the kingdom of God and how that kingdom was so alternative to the kingdom Israel had previously experienced.

We should follow Jesus' example. Jesus said he was going to send his spirit and when his spirit came, what was the first thing that happened? Racial, ethnic, and cultural barriers were broken. Look at this passage in Acts 2:5–11:

> At that time there were devout Jews from every nation living in Jerusalem. When they heard the loud noise, everyone came running, and they were bewildered to hear their own languages being spoken by the believers. They were completely amazed. "How can this be?" they

exclaimed. "These people are all from Galilee, and yet we hear them speaking in our own native languages! Here we are—Parthians, Medes, Elamites, people from Mesopotamia, Judea, Cappadocia, Pontus, the province of Asia, Phrygia, Pamphylia, Egypt, and the areas of Libya around Cyrene, visitors from Rome (both Jews and converts to Judaism), Cretans, and Arabs. And we all hear these people speaking in our own languages about the wonderful things God has done!

Instead of living with the scarcity mentality, pigeonholed in a homogenous world, surrounded by people who are like us. We generously invest in friendships with people that are not like us. The Gospel gives us the power to bridge divides, break down barriers, invest, encourage, and build with people who look differently, act differently, think differently, are from different cultures and neighborhoods and ethnicities.

Jesus gave us the ability to bridge the divide with God and with our fellow man through the cross. The good news about Jesus is that He is the bridge. Look what they said in Acts they were declaring the wonderful things God had done!

The power of the Gospel is its ability to be radically inclusive. Jesus was radically exclusive. He said I am the only way to the Father, but in the same breath he was radically inclusive. And in his great love, a great exchange takes place.

When you give God your heart, He fills it with love instead of hate.

When you hand God regrets, He will hand you back hope.

When you hand God transgressions, He will hand you back forgiveness.

When you hand God rebellion, He will hand you back peace.

When you hand God restlessness, He will hand you back tranquility.

When you hand God fear, He will hand you back courage.

When you hand God your insecurity, He will hand you confidence.

When you hand God your prejudice, He will hand you a desire for unity/harmony.

The power of the Gospel gives us grace to take the wrongs we experienced, those horrific events that happened to us, and instead of letting them ruin our image and turn us into something ugly and full of pain, can instead transform us into a beautiful tapestry that like a renowned artist so proudly renders to the world, God proudly shows to a deteriorating culture, to a fallen world, not to show off but to inspire and stir and urge and convince and convict the lost and people living in darkness to turn and be found to live in the light.

That's what grace does. It is resilient, rising, buoyant, an upward force! And it cancels the weight and gravity of sin that would otherwise drown us. Seeing the love of God in the glory of Christ is what restructures our hearts and we ordered our desires. The size of God breaks the power of sin over our hearts. Remember, my friends, one heart can cause tremendous devastation or great healing. It matters what happens in one heart and in one mind. We will not curse the darkness in our society we will instead declare the light.

To repeat what Dr. Martin Luther King, Jr. said on September 18, 1963 in response to four little girls that died from a bomb planted at Sixteenth Street Baptist Church:

"Now I say to you in conclusion, life is hard, at times as hard as crucible steel. It has its bleak and difficult moments. Like the ever-flowing waters of the river, life has its moments of drought and its moments of flood. Like the ever-changing cycle of the seasons, life has the soothing warmth of its summers and the piercing chill of its winters. And one will hold on, you will discover that God walks with him and that God is able to lift you from the fatigue of despair to the buoyancy of hope, and transform dark and desolate valleys into sunlight passive inner peace."

My Heart Breaks for Baton Rouge

It was eerie to wake up and see Baton Rouge in the national spotlight yesterday, making headlines on all the major news outlets and trending as the number one topic on Twitter. The story? Alton Sterling, a thirty-seven-year-old black man, was fatally shot at point-blank range by two Baton Rouge police officers. I was going to post this blog late last night, but I decided to wait and post it this morning. I was shocked and devastated to wake up this morning with more headline news—a livestream Facebook video of Philando Castile, shot by a police officer and dying on the scene, was on the home page of CNN. What happened in Baton Rouge hits close to home—as a former resident and city employee, my heart grieves for the capitol city. I spent years working to revitalize many of Baton Rouge's traditionally disinvested communities (including the neighborhood where Sterling was killed).

Second, as an African American pastor ministering in a predominantly white congregation, I'm often asked questions on race relations in America. People are genuinely searching for answers on this exceptionally sensitive subject and are looking for someone to help them navigate their thoughts and subsequent response as a Christ follower. Finally, as a doctoral student at Duke University, tragedies like Alton Sterling and Philando Castile's deaths have compelled me to write my doctoral thesis on racial reconciliation in America. It's important to thoughtfully, constructively, and civilly address issues that affect the social, political, and religious landscape of America and give direction on how we can pray and act in the wake of this tragedy. What happened in Baton

Rouge and Minneapolis has, yet again, aggravated the deep wound of racial conflict and misunderstanding in America. So where do we go from here? America is reeling from these tragedies.

Below is a list of practical things you can do to be a part of the arduous task of racial reconciliation in America.

It's imperative that we empathize with the pain of Sterling and Castile's families.

We need to stop for a second and imagine the pain they are going through. Empathy involves you being aware of, sensitive to, and vicariously experiencing the feelings, thoughts, and experiences of another of either the past or present without having the feelings, thoughts, and experience fully communicated in an objective manner. You may not be able to articulate the pain of these families, but it's necessary that you seek to put yourself in their shoes.

My eyes were blurred with tears as I watched Alton Sterling's fifteen-year-old son sob during a press conference on the death of his father. Can you imagine what he's going through? Can you put yourself in his shoes? He lost his father. Tracy and I watched the video of Castile's death this morning and I had to leave the room because I was completely overwhelmed with emotion. Can you feel the level of loss that their families are experiencing, knowing that the death of their loved ones is now in the national spotlight with millions of people venting their frustrations and opinions?

There is an immense amount of pain that is being felt among family and friends. Before we pray for healing, I think it would be prudent to take a time and reflect on how deep this wound is for their family, friends, and community.

Pray for the Pastors in Baton Rouge and Minneapolis

Let us pray specifically that God will give them wisdom in addressing their congregations and grace to lead in the weeks, months, and years to come. There will undoubtedly be confusion and questions that arise in congregations across Minneapolis and Baton Rouge.

We need to pray for the Spirit of Wisdom and Revelation to infuse pastors' hearts and minds. I love Walter Brueggemann's line: "nurture, nourish, and evoke a consciousness that is alternative to the perception of the dominant culture around us."[clxv] My prayer is that pastors would speak with conviction and authority on God's salvific hope and healing power and that what they would stand in stark contrast to what is presently happening in the hearts and minds of the people in Baton Rouge and Minneapolis. That hope, faith, and healing would replace confusion, strife, and division.

We Need to Pray for the Police Officers in Baton Rouge and Minneapolis

Day after day, thousands of police officers put their life on the line to protect the citizens in Baton Rouge and Minneapolis. A majority of them are good men and women. We need to pray against any retaliation against them. We need to pray that God would use them as agents of healing and that God would supernaturally move in the hearts and minds of men and women who harbor bitterness or resentment against them.

There's nothing wrong with being angry at what has happened and seeking reformation in the police department, but we need to remember that a majority of law enforcement officers are good people, with good hearts, and want to do the right thing.

Pray for the Churches in Baton Rouge and Minneapolis

We need to pray for the churches across these two cities, that from their hallowed halls would spring an outpouring of the love and grace of God. I pray that the church would rise and lead the process of restoration and reconciliation in these cities. That ministries across Baton Rouge and Minneapolis would find a new source of strength to be the hands and feet of Jesus in this dark time.

Pray that God will use these Tragedies to Bring about a Renewed Effort of Racial Reconciliation

We know the typical narrative that two sides of this issue espouse. One that emphasizes consistent police brutality toward minorities in major metropolitan areas. The other side highlights the systemic violence that plagues African American neighborhoods, that "all lives matter," and that this culture of violence is not addressed with the same amount of energy as police brutality. Why can't we believe that God can use this tragedy to ignite a whole new level of restoration and healing in the cities? Why do we have to resort to strife and division when events like this happen? Why do we use heated rhetoric and drive-by social media posts to demonize others who don't hold up our opinion? We need to pray and fast that God would break through calloused hearts and mend racial wounds in Baton Rouge, Minneapolis, and America. Why can't we choose to be an instrument of healing, peace, and love, not strife and confusion?

Engage in Cross-Cultural Interaction

There are many barriers that divide us: age, appearance, intelligence, political persuasion, economic status, race, theological perspective. One of the best ways to stifle Christ's Love is to be friendly with only those people that we like. We tend to befriend and connect with people who are culturally similar to us. This creates and maintains a homogenous lifestyle where one fails to have a diverse set of friends and voices in their life. Connect with people that are different from you. Particularly, ethnically different from you. If you are white, talk to a black person about police brutality. If you are black, develop relationships with your white brothers and sisters and don't be afraid to talk about the political and cultural issues that are important to you.

Listen Actively

If we're going to experience true racial reconciliation in this country, we're going have to resolve to listen well to the "other" side. To listen well, you have to be transparent. Being honest in your communication is essential to creating trust. Vulnerability and transparency break down barriers. We don't communicate effectively because of fear; we don't open up out of trepidation of rejection or apprehension from getting hurt. But when you're transparent and vulnerable, you go a long way to alleviate the concerns and fears of that other person you're communicating with. Be intentional in your conversation. Ask questions. If you want to cultivate a healthy relationship, you must be conscientious in your dialogue.

150

Be Willing to Yield on Some of Your Views

Arrogance breeds dogmatism. It is important to stand up for what you believe in. We must be a people of deep conviction, but don't be so dogmatic in your position that you can never see or seek to understand a contrasting opinion. When we are overly dogmatic in the defense of our position we tend to cause another person's defensive walls to go up . Once those walls are up, it can be quite difficult to really hear the other's point of view.

Personally Acknowledge and Embrace the Arduous Task of Reconciliation

Let's not put a band aid on this issue. Pray for wisdom for city leaders and for justice to prevail in the federal investigation. We need to recognize that this issue is not going to be fixed overnight. It's going to take many conversations, prayers, and active outreach. It's going to take changes in government policy. It's going to take forgiveness. Please don't move on after a couple of days or weeks. Actively participate in racial reconciliation. Ask your pastors and mentors what you can do to be a part of the solution.

Reject Color Blindness

There is a dominant ideology that many believe solves racism. I categorically reject color blindness...and you should too. Austin Channing helpfully diagnoses this attitude: "Believing in the notion of colorblindness sounds like this, 'I don't even see color,' or this, 'But we are all the same,' or this, 'I've never looked at you as a (fill in the blank).' These statements are usually followed by a sugary example of our sameness and ends with a quote by Martin Luther King, Jr.

about character not color being what REALLY counts."[clxvi]

One can be pro–black lives *and* pro-humanity. Why do we have to rush and quote #AllLivesMatter when we see a #BlackLivesMatter on a social media post? You can notice my race and still acknowledge my humanity. I acknowledge that my wife is a white woman. She clearly knows that I am a black man. And we have embraced our cultural and ethnic differences. "Too many people have bought into the myth that to see color is to erase my humanity, my character, my individuality. When actually my race can give you clues into who I am, if I am given the chance to explain why my race matters."[clxvii]

I encourage you to reject colorblindness and become color conscious. Colorblindness disregards ethnic differences, but such disregard doesn't make these differences go away. Color consciousness makes one aware of race and celebrates the differences. This ideology compels us to acknowledge, embrace, and celebrate ethnic differences. It appreciates diverse thoughts, perspectives, and regularly seeks them out.

Read Dr. Martin Luther King's "Letter from a Birmingham Jail"

This is perhaps the most powerful piece of literature I have read besides the Bible. I would encourage you to take twenty minutes to read and reflect on King's passionate plea to fight racism in America. It will give you great insight into the problem of race in America. Let's take the lead on this issue, folks. I'll leave you with this inspiring quote: "If there are those who fuel the fire, there are also those who douse the flames."

PART FOUR

RENEWAL

Institutional Mitigation of Racialized Tragedies

REALIZATION

RENEWAL

RACIAL CRISIS
FRAMEWORK

READINESS

RESPONSIVENESS

The final part of the Racial Crisis Framework is renewal. Here, I focus on how racialized crises can be catalytic events that spur needed organizational reorientation and change. Renewal challenges faith leaders and congregations to radically reorient who they are and how they do church after a racialized storm. Renewal is all about learning and implementing changes so that churches can become resilient institutions in the face of a changing sociopolitical climate.

Church leaders must harness the energy these crises bring and use it to their advantage. What is the advantage to racial discord and division? The advantage is that millions of people across America are talking about the issue. Whether the removal of the confederate flag, confederate statues, NFL players kneeling during the national anthem, or an unarmed black man being gunned down by police, these situations force the nation to talk about race.

Discussions about race are typically difficult because blacks and whites often come from opposite perspectives. America has a problem with racism, but it also has a problem of amnesia. Americans tend to forget how severe and pervasive racism (both interpersonal and systemic) was and continues to be in this country. Michael Eric Dyson comments on the proclivity of whites to forget about how prevalent racism is in America. He writes,

> It seems impossible to pull off, but many of you appear to live in what the late writer and cultural critic Gore Vidal called "The United States of Amnesia." When black folk get in your face, or even just expect you to know a little about black life, to take the past into account when speaking about black life, your reaction is often, simply, to forget it. It is a willful refusal to know...White America, you deliberately forget how whiteness caused black suffering. And it shows in the strangest ways. You forget how you kept black folk poor as sharecroppers. You forget how you kept us out of your classrooms and in subpar schools. You forget how you denied us jobs, and when we got them, how you denied us promotions. You forget how you kept us out of the suburbs, and now that you're gentrifying our inner-city neighborhoods, you're pushing us out to the suburbs. You forget that you kept us from voting, and then blamed us for being lackadaisical at the polls.[clxviii]

Dyson goes on to argue that this amnesia isn't limited to conservative white politicians, but is pervasive in our culture. The concept of collective amnesia applies to racialized crises. An event captures and captivates news media and social media outlets, a public outcry is made, but the event and subsequent issues it brings up eventually fades into the background amid the noise of a twenty-four-hour news cycle. Church leaders must realize they have small window of time to respond to these events. The renewal section makes the case that these storms are opportunities for leaders to challenge prevailing prejudicial attitudes in our congregation and communities.

VIII

Racialized Crises as Catalytic Events

That is the resilience dividend. It means more than effectively returning to normal functioning after a disruption, although that is critical. It is about achieving significant transformation that yields benefits even when disruptions are not.

—JUDITH RODIN, *THE RESILIENCE DIVIDEND*

This book has repeatedly emphasized the points that racialized crises are disruptive, generate unrest, and lead to division and tension within congregations and communities. While there are policies, that if implemented, could reduce the severity, frequency, and intensity of these crises, Americans will always have to deal with traumatic racial events in a multi-ethnic, pluralistic democracy. However, instead of collectively wringing our hands and resorting to cynicism and fatalism, institutions and individuals can choose to do something about these storms.

Climatologists and emergency management officials do not give up and resign themselves to inaction in the face of rising sea levels and intense hurricanes. They plan, strategize, assess, organize, implement, monitor, evaluate, and prepare. Church leaders must do the same. We must change our perspective about racialized crises. Instead of seeing them through the lens of despair and helplessness, we must begin to see them as catalytic events that can potentially lead to needed organizational change and renewal. These events have the potential to lead to revitalization, to clear the individual or institution's canvas. Judith Rodin argues that revitalization after a disruption is a positive for an organization:

> Revitalization is the process of bringing new life and vigor to an individual, an organization, or a community after it has been through a disruption, a crisis, a disaster. Revitalization goes beyond the achievement of bouncing forward. It suggests that natural systems surge toward greater robustness than ever, that infrastructure performs to high expectations, that communities gain strength, people are energized,

identity is enriched, and a shared vision, takes shape.[clxix]

It is common to hear the phrase "bounce back" when talking about recovery from a major storm. Public discourse has focused on how to get these communities to bounce back from the storms. However, what would it look like, instead of bouncing back, if these communities bounced forward? What have these communities learned about planning, vulnerability, storm readiness, and recovery? What resilience measures would be implemented now by city officials, having experienced devastation from major hurricanes? Change is not easy. It often takes a major disruption to generate the transformation needed to make individuals and institutions stronger, buoyant, and resistant to storms. That is why it is vital for church leaders to look at these racialized storms as change agents that can potentially propel a church forward by years in a few months' time.

The weight and pull of the status quo is always a powerful force in the life of any institution. Salter-McNeil comments on how social and cultural enclaves lead to institutional inertia when it comes to organizational change that focuses on racial reconciliation. These social and ethnic enclaves essentially become echo chambers that reaffirm and reinforce the positions and attitudes that have shaped our constructed social reality. She writes:

> These social and cultural enclaves to which we cling are our places of refuge. The world makes sense to us there, and our identity is affirmed when we are in close proximity with those who are most like us and share our values. The other people in our group mirror who we are and socialize us to believe certain things about

> ourselves and others. We see ourselves reflected there,
> and the rituals and customs that bond us together make
> us feel safe and comfortable.[clxx]

McNeil-Salter suggests that all of us are predisposed to ethnocentrism, a sociological term that "denotes belief in the inherent superiority of one's own ethnic group or culture."[clxxi] The proclivity to ethnocentrism prevents congregations from engaging in the work of racial inclusion, justice, equity, and reconciliation. "The pull of our human tendencies toward self-focus and preservation is too strong and ultimately, albeit slowly, draws us from the refining process of becoming reconcilers."[clxxii] Catalytic events can lead individuals and institutions down the road to isolation and preservation, or on the path to reconciliation and organizational transformation.

The aim for church leaders is to harness the disruption caused by tragic events for needed organizational and communal change: the anger, fear, tension, division, are all catalysts. A catalyst is something that has enormous amount of energy. That energy can be used to disrupt the long-standing systems, processes, and cultural norms that have made organizations susceptible and vulnerable to racialized crises.

> This is what catalytic events have the potential to do to us. Catalytic events allow us to move from the isolation and stagnation of life in homogenous groups and break through into a new reality that introduces us to something we have never experienced before.[clxxiii]
>
> The word catalyst comes from the Greek words katalysis and katalyein, which literally mean to dissolve and loosen. Considering these terms

scientifically, if we want to bring about the chemical reaction required for dissolution, it is necessary to decrease or loosen the strength of a chemical bond, or to increase the energy to overcome that bond...A catalyst can work by altering the activation energy of a reaction or the amount of energy needed for a reaction. It agitates the atoms, encouraging them to bump into each other more often and thus to form new molecular arrangements or relationships...Without the help of a catalyst, chemical reactions might never occur; then there can be no new arrangement of molecules.[clxxiv]

The goal is to find balance in the disruption. Too much, and the organization suffers from irreparable damage; too little, and the organization does not get the necessary jumpstart needed to spur change in entrenched ways.

Adaptive Leadership

Ronald Heifetz addresses this balance in his book, *Leadership Without Easy Answers*. Heifetz defines leadership as an activity rather than a set of personality traits or a position of authority.[clxxv] It is imperative, he argues, that leaders engage in what he calls "adaptive work," which "consists of the learning required to address conflicts in the values people hold, or to diminish the gap between the values people stand for and the reality they face."[clxxvi] Heifetz writes that typically, society reacts to issues in three different ways. The first way is to utilize a response that has worked well in the past. The second is to meet new challenges by using familiar solutions. The third response is to engage in adaptive work where individuals and institutions learn new methods to tackle issues.

Heifetz distinguishes between technical solutions and adaptive solutions. A technical solution is quick, expedient work that quickly resolves an issue. In times of crises, people look to leaders for technical solutions. We often want "experts" to give us fast and accurate answers when confronted with complex challenges. When it comes to racialized storms, however, the solution will not be quick. Mitigating the disruption caused by racialized storms requires comprehensive, holistic, and adaptive changes. Salter-McNeil comments on how pain can lead to lasting change:

> Change can be painful and coercive because we cannot control or manage it. Conversion and comprehensive change is arduous, difficult and often very slow, because it requires us to give up long-held beliefs and assumptions. That is why it often takes a catalytic event in our lives to force us out of our space of comfort and into new spaces of growth and transformation.[clxxvii]

It is vital that faith leaders understand and make the appropriate distinction between technical solutions and adaptive work. Faith leaders must engage in adaptive work to truly confront the complexity and reality of deteriorating race relations in America. Adaptive leadership compels people to tackle tough challenges, to change as new circumstances and problems arise, and to tackle those issues with new strategies and abilities.

> Transformation requires disruption and a degree of chaos to increase the sense of urgency that change must happen. However, there must also be enough psychological safety that the chaos does not completely

overwhelm our ability to reflect and reorganize ourselves. A catalytic event will either push us forward toward transformation or tighten our tether to preservation. I have seen strategies that were stressful enough to create change but ultimately were not safe enough to allow people to form new patters. On the other hand, I've also seen educational strategies that allowed for safe spaces for open dialogue but did not create enough discomfort to push a group's members beyond their old patterns of relating. There must be both![clxxviii]

Adaptive leadership must be exercised to mitigate the disruption from traumatic racial events. Faith leaders must understand that exercising leadership in this area is risky and difficult. Instead of providing every answer, leaders would be wise to provide questions, or enable their congregation to face the hard facts about racialized storms. Churches need to be confronted with reality, but not overwhelmed by it.

One key principle of adaptive leadership, Heifctz explains, is to keep levels of distress within a tolerable range. He draws on the concept of "holding environment," a method to keep levels of distress within an endurable range. The term,

originated in psychoanalysis to describe the relationship between the therapist and the patient. The therapist "holds" the patient in a process of developmental learning in a way that has some similarities to the way a mother and father hold their newborn and maturing children...To be effective, therapists have to empathize and understand their patients' struggles so that the patients can begin to see more clearly the nature of their problems.[clxxix]

The point is to introduce stress in measurable ways to introduce incremental change in the people's attitudes and beliefs. Adaptive leadership involves telling people what they don't want to hear to engage in the work that they desperately need in their lives and organizations. The holding environment "consists of any relationship in which one party has the power to hold the attention of another party and facilitate adaptive work."[clxxx] Whatever strategies faith leaders implement to prepare their churches for racialized crises, they must take into account the process of incremental change. Attitudes, beliefs, and ways of living do not change overnight. A balance must be attained.

Heifetz uses the example of a pressure cooker to show that the point of the holding environment is not to eliminate the stress. The stress of implementing these strategies is needed for a church if they truly want to lead during crises and work toward racial unity. The goal is to bring greater awareness to the ways that racialized events disrupt churches, communities, and cities.

> People cannot learn new ways when they are overwhelmed. But eliminating stress altogether eliminates the impetus for adaptive work. The strategic task is to maintain a level of tension that mobilizes people. To return to our pressure-cooker metaphor, the cook regulates the pressure of the holding environment by turning the heat up or down, while the relief valve lets off steam to keep the pressure within a safe limit. If the pressure goes beyond the carrying capacity of the vessel, the pressure cooker can blow up. On the other hand, with no heat nothing cooks.[clxxxi]

The point, in fact, is to turn up the heat. When it comes to the work of racial reconciliation, too often, faith leaders abandon the process because the issue inevitably brings up tension. Discomfort is a natural part of change. People in positions of authority have an inherent advantage in generating the distress. They have control over the decision-making process and have the power to direct the attention of their congregation toward a specific issue.

I have always appreciated the definition Nan Keohane (Professor at the Institute for Advanced Study at Princeton University) offers in her magisterial book, *Thinking About Leadership*. She defines leadership as "providing solutions to common problems or offering ideas about how to accomplish collective purposes, and mobilizing the energies of others to follow these courses of action."[clxxxii] Her definition reminds us that leadership is essentially communal and relies upon marshaling the resources and energy of other people to achieve certain outcomes.

Renewal is a key component of the Racial Crisis Framework. There is a tendency, on the part of many church leaders, to avoid the adaptive work that congregations and communities desperately need. However, to gather the energy and momentum needed to sustain the journey along the framework, church leaders need to see how their organizations can renew and revitalize from these storms. "Resilient entities—those with high levels of awareness sufficient readiness, and the capacity to effectively respond—move on. Not only do they bounce back to a functioning state, they bounce forward."[clxxxiii]

Learning and reflecting in the aftermath of a racial crisis

enables church leaders to lead better when the next racialized crisis occurs. Too often, church leaders want to move quickly past the disruption and unrest that these storms bring. Understandably, racialized crises produce anger, tension, division, civil unrest, and threaten the fabric of social cohesion in any organization. Nevertheless, when church leaders adopt the strategy of bouncing back quickly, congregations miss a moment to teach individuals and churches about the pain that people on the margins are feeling when these storms strike.

Natural disasters have a peculiar way of getting people's attention and forcing them to face the reality of how they live. Once a racialized crisis strikes, church leaders should look at the event to help their congregations understand the hard historical and present-day truths about race in America.

Church leaders need to manage the holding environment and resist the proclivity of wanting to get back to normal. The renewal section challenges this philosophy of "getting back to normal" and encourages pastors to utilize the disruption to accomplish significant organizational change in their churches and communities. Kathleen Tierney observes:

> Learning and changes do sometimes take place in the aftermath of disasters, often because disasters open policy windows, by forcing key actors to acknowledge long-standing problems, by revealing unanticipated threats, and by temporarily suppressing forces that support the status quo. For example, after the 1933 Long Beach earthquake, which caused severe damage to school buildings, the state of California passed the Field Act, which mandated seismically safe construction for public schools...Some communities do learn from

disasters, even if many do not. After experiencing a series of severe floods, the city of Tulsa, Oklahoma, embarked in the 1980s on an ambitious flood mitigation program that is now recognized as a model of its kind.[clxxxiv]

Renewal looks at a racialized storm as an opportunity to grow from and seek lasting change. These storms give church leaders an opportunity to challenge long-standing and false narratives about people of color and America's innocence in matters of race.

Racialized crises give church leaders an opening to mobilize their congregations to tackle the tough adaptive work in communities instead of remaining in their safe walls. American will always have racialized tension, division, and disruption. However, we can choose to respond. We can choose to engage in work that helps heal our land.

What can contemporary American Christian leaders do in the face of deteriorating race relations in America? How can they respond to the sociopolitical unrest? Church leaders must be truth-tellers who are grounded in moral clarity and conviction, grounded in social awareness, narrative-driven, engage in prophetic imagination, and effectively deploy lament. Faith leaders must mobilize their congregations to be beacons of justice, equality, reconciliation in a dark and divisive world.

Conclusion

Fifty-two years ago, future United States Senator Daniel Patrick Moynihan wrote a report on the conditions of the black family in America. Moynihan, then an aide in the Department of Labor, was suspicious about the progress of black advancement in the civil rights era. Though a proponent of the Civil Rights Movement, Moynihan didn't feel that the legislation of the 1964 Civil Rights Act and federal policy was enough to alleviate the pain and suffering that black families faced as a result of hundreds of years of white oppression. Coates writes,

> Moynihan began searching for a way to press the point within the Johnson administration. "I felt like I had to write a paper about the Negro family," Moynihan later recalled, "to explain to the fellows how there was a problem more difficult than they knew." In March 1965, Moynihan printed up one hundred copies of a report he and a small staff had labored over for only a few months. The report was called "The Negro Family: The Case for National Action"...Running against the tide of optimism around the civil rights, "The Negro Family" argued that the federal government was underestimating the damage done to black families by "three centuries of sometimes unimaginable mistreatment" as well as a "racist virus in the American bloodstream," which would continue to plague blacks in the future.[clxxxv]

Moynihan's report was received with enthusiasm among President Lyndon Johnson's advisors. He was soon recruited to write President Johnson's major speech on race relations to Howard University's graduating class in June of

1965.clxxxvi Moynihan's rise continued throughout the 1960s. Additionally, several race riots, in the mid– and late 1960s, contributed to Moynihan's ascent. The 1965 Watts riots in Los Angeles occurred just months after Moynihan's report. Los Angeles burned for nearly a week. Nearly three dozen people died and the area sustained tens of millions in damages.clxxxvii The Watts riots, like Ferguson nearly fifty years later, fundamentally shook America's sociopolitical landscape.

While Moynihan's report was heavily criticized for being too patriarchal and condescending to black families, he nonetheless continued to occupy high posts in both the Johnson and Nixon administrations. He soon ran for the U.S. senate and won, representing the state of New York for decades. What launched Moynihan into political stardom was his groundbreaking report, which, interestingly enough, gave no policy recommendations.

James Patterson writes on Moynihan's report: "His report was diagnostic, not a blueprint for cure. Seeking to stimulate the formation of carefully planned and well-informed governmental policies, Moynihan did not provide a wish list of proposed solutions."clxxxviii Moynihan wanted his work to stimulate a national conversation about the socioeconomic conditions of the black family. Could we really expect, as a country, for black families to truly be equal to white families after several hundred years of oppression and discrimination? His report stressed the urgency of national action.

This book—while grounded in sociological analysis, psychological concepts, theories of climate change adaptation, natural disaster mitigation policies, presidential politics, theological inquiry, and biblical exegesis—aims at more than simply stimulating a conversation about race relations (though a robust and honest dialogue about the condition of race in America is needed in institutions across America). My hope is to provide faith leaders with a toolkit that mitigates racial tension and division in their own congregations and subsequently in their own communities and cities. Each part of the Racial Crisis Framework— Realization, Readiness, Responsiveness, and Renewal—must first be implemented in a church's own backyard. Church leaders cannot hope to lead effectively during times of racialized crisis that divide America if their own organizations are riddled with ethnic strife, division, or are bastions of homogeneity. This framework seeks to aid pastors in raising awareness, preparing for, responding to, and renewing from the next racialized crisis by actively working toward racial equality and reconciliation before the storm hits.

The overarching methods in the framework are broad and that is intentional. Every church is unique, positioned in a community for "such a time as this." This book aims not to hold contemporary Christian leaders' hands, but to make the case, like Moynihan's report did over fifty years ago, that urgent action is required to close the racial divide that endures today. Church leaders must make the framework an institutional priority in their congregation. Intentionally prioritizing the framework, as a value of the church, is critical to the framework's sustainability and effectiveness.

Moynihan's report placed faith "in the marriage of government and social science to formulate policy" that would solve America's generational legacy of racial inequality.[clxxxix] I've worked in the government arena and, like Moynihan, believe in the power of national policy action. However, the church is unlike any institution in America. The church has been entrusted with the task of communicating this glorious news of Jesus Christ's mission to redeem all of creation. This book is aimed primarily at the church, because I believe in the church as a conduit for God's mercy, love, compassion, and justice to flow to a broken and dark world.

Acknowledgments

In the liner notes section of his 1964 groundbreaking album *A Love Supreme*, world-renowned jazz artist John Coltrane wrote, "This album is a humble offering to Him. An attempt to say, 'THANK YOU GOD' through our work, even as we do in our hearts and with our tongues." Coltrane couldn't have said it better. I feel the same about this book. It is a humble offering to God, who has inspired me to write, sustained me through the difficult times, and placed key people in my life to see me to the finish line. God has been so gracious and merciful throughout this entire process.

I'm thankful to Duke University and Duke Divinity School for the opportunity to pursue my doctoral studies. It has been a dream come true to attend Duke and I'm proud to forever be a Dukie. I am deeply grateful for the support of my advisor, Bishop Will Willimon. Bishop is literally a living legend. I remember being mesmerized at how he taught during the program. His recent book, *Who Lynched Willie Earle?: Preaching to Confront Racism*, was an enormous inspiration as I wrote this book. More than Bishop's timeliness in responding to my numerous inquiries or his vast knowledge from the nearly seventy books he's written, I'm grateful for his belief in me. He gave me confidence that what I was writing on was critical to the church today.

There are several other faculty members who have been important to me on this journey. Craig Hill (who has gone on to become the dean of Southern Methodist University's Perkins School of Theology) was the director of the DMin program at Duke when I first enrolled. I'm thankful for his humor, wit, and belief that I would be a valuable addition to

172

the 2015 cohort. Jenn Graffius, Alice Wade, Mark Won, and Tim Mentzer were immensely helpful throughout the program at Duke.

Allison Chandler continues to loom large over my academic career. She was a student advisor assigned to me by the athletic department at the University of North Florida nearly fifteen years ago. She was patient, kind, and unwavering in her conviction that I was a gifted student and needed to see myself as that. I shall forever remain indebted to her. She literally dreamed for me.

I will always be thankful for The Young Professionals ministry at Southpoint Community Church. I started this journey during my time as a pastor to that group. I am grateful for their prayers and support. It was one of the greatest joys in my life to serve as their pastor. Thank you for teaching me what true diversity, inclusion, and brotherly love looks like. I'm thankful to my best friends, Jon Greer and Derrick Roberts, for the late-night talks and laughs.

The humor of Stephen Colbert, Trevor Noah, Seth Meyers, and Rickey Smiley (playing Sister Bernice Jenkins) has been life-giving these past couple of years. Hans Zimmer's Interstellar soundtrack has literally been instrumental to me during this entire experience. I must have listened to it hundreds of times. For some odd reason, it has been a tradition for me to watch Christopher Nolan's film Interstellar after finishing every final paper during the last three years. Nolan is a cinematic genius and Interstellar is one of those films that continues to inspire me.

My mom and dad have been wonderful. My mom first fanned the flame of my passion for history, race relations, and politics by requiring me to read biographies, autobiographies, and history books on African Americans. She has always believed in me and pushed me to shoot for the stars. My dad is brilliant. I always looked up to him and enjoyed our conversations on politics in America. Those chats helped to sharpen my mind and think critically on the serious issues that our country faces today. I'm immensely thankful for my brother-in-law, Fabrice Juin. Our conversations sparked numerous ideas that went into this book. He's a good man and I'm better that he's in our family. My sister Deanna has been my compass. Always pointing me toward true North. I'm grateful for her. My brother, David, has a way of making me laugh like few humans. I love him dearly.

My family has played a pivotal role in this thesis. My sons, Luke and Noah Briscoe, are old enough to know when Daddy's gone. Countless times, they've asked, "Where is Daddy?" to which my loving wife would reply, "Daddy's studying at Duke, but don't worry, he'll be home soon." I love my boys. They bring me great joy. I just love watching them. I'm grateful for how each one contributes his own unique element to our family. I'm thankful for Luke's exuberance and Noah's sensitivity. Boys, Daddy loves you forever. My daughters, Amelia Hope and Ella Grace, are my treasures. They truly bring out the colors of life.

Finally, my extraordinary wife, Tracy, has made inestimable sacrifices. She has endured countless late nights and early mornings with our children. She has been my biggest encourager. She has fought, defended, celebrated, and loved me through this entire process. I could not have asked for a better cheerleader. I appreciate her always being available to talk through ideas regarding the content of the book. Tracy has been exceedingly patient and long suffering when I had to take time away from the family to research and write. I love you, Tracy.

About the Author

Dr. Harold Dorrell Briscoe is a writer, speaker, pastor, and public theologian. He focuses on the intersectionality of race, religion, law, and power. He is married to Tracy, and a father to Luke, Noah, Amelia Hope, and Ella Grace.

He is a 2007 graduate of the University of North Florida where he earned his bachelor's degree in Political Science and History. He is a 2009 graduate of the George Bush School of Government and Public Service at Texas A&M University. There he earned a master's degree in Public Administration with a concentration on Urban Planning. Dorrell worked in local and state government for five years, across Florida, Texas, and Louisiana.

Dorrell also taught at the university level as an adjunct professor teaching public administration, management, and leadership to undergraduate students. While teaching, Dorrell pursued and was awarded a master's degree in Theological Studies at Liberty University in 2015.

Dorrell finished his Doctor of Ministry degree at Duke University in 2017. He has a strong passion for the local church, politics, racial justice, equality and international affairs.

He is the founder and Lead Pastor of The Six:Eight Church in Durham, North Carolina. Six:Eight's vision is to build a gospel community that is intentionally diverse, cross-cultural, and neighborhood-centered by engaging and developing ministries in Downtown Durham and the Hayti Community.

Notes

[i] I have coined this term and will use it throughout the paper to describe racially charged events in America. Chapter 2 will discuss this concept in more detail.

[ii] Brenda Salter McNeil, *Roadmap to Reconciliation* (Downers Grove: InterVarsity Press, 2015), 17.

[iii] Federal Emergency Management Glossary, https://training.fema.gov/emiweb/is/icsresource/assets/icsglossary.pdf (accessed August 23, 2017).

[iv] Matthew 19:26, NIV.

[v] United Nations, "Framework Convention on Climate Change," May 31, 2017, http://unfccc.int/paris_agreement/items/9485.php.

[vi] Stefan Becket, "Paris Climate Agreement: What You Need to Know," CBS News, Accessed June 1, 2017, https://www.cbsnews.com/news/paris-climate-agreement-what-you-need-to-know/.

[vii] "Climate Change: How Do We Know?" Global Climate Change: Vital Signs of the Planet, last modified November 6, 2017, https://climate.nasa.gov/evidence/.

[viii] Ibid.

[ix] Ibid.

[x] Briscoe, Adaptation to Climate Change in the Houston-Galveston Area.

[xi] Ibid.

[xii] "Robert F. Kennedy Predicted Black Presidency to the Exact Year," *Rollingout*, last modified December 25, 2008, https://rollingout.com/2008/12/25/robert-f-kennedy-predicted-black-presidency-to-the-exact-year/.

[xiii] Tim Wise, Between Barack and a Hard Place: Racism and

White Denial in the Age of Obama. (San Francisco: City lights Books, 2009), 7.

xiv "Disgraceful: Cops Angry After Obama Slams Arrest of Black Scholar," *Fox News*, last modified July 24, 2009, http://www.foxnews.com/story/2009/07/24/disgraceful-cops-angry-after-obama-slams-arrest-black-scholar.html.

xv Peniel Joseph, "Obama's Efforts to Heal Racial Divisions and Uplift Black America," *The Washington Post,* last modified April 22, 2016, https://www.washingtonpost.com/graphics/national/obama-legacy/racism-during-presidency.html.

xvi "Remarks By the President on Trayvon Martin," *The White House: Office of the Press Secretary*, July 19, 2013, https://obamawhitehouse.archives.gov/the-press-office/2013/07/19/remarks-president-trayvon-martin

xvii Tom Cohen, "Obama: 'Trayvon Martin Could Have Been Me,'" *CNN Politics*, last modified July 19, 2013, http://www.cnn.com/2013/07/19/politics/obama-zimmerman/index.html.

xviii William Frey, "New Projections Point to a Majority Minority Nation in 2044," *Brookings*, last modified December 12, 2014, https://www.brookings.edu/blog/the-avenue/2014/12/12/new-projections-point-to-a-majority-minority-nation-in-2044/

xix Catherine Woodiwiss, "The Era of White Anxiety Is Just Beginning," *Sojourner*, last modified March 8, 2016, https://sojo.net/articles/era-white-anxiety-just-beginning

xx Ibid.

xxi Ibid.

xxii Amanda Taub, "White Nationalism, Explained," *New York Times*, last modified November 21, 2016, https://www.nytimes.com/2016/11/22/world/americas/white-nationalism-explained.html?mcubz=1.

xxiii Candice Smith, "Some White Trump Supporters Fear Becoming Minority," *ABC News*, last modified November 2, 2016, http://abcnews.go.com/Politics/white-trump-supporters-fear-minority/story?id=43229203.

xxiv Cassandra Chaney and Danielle Joy Davis, "No Justice, No Peace: Social Unrest in Ferguson," *The Western Journal of Black Studies* 39, no. 4 (2015): 268.

xxv Marc Lamont Hill, Nobody: Casualties of America's War on the Vulnerable, from Ferguson to Flint and Beyond (New York: Atria Paperback, 2017), 11-12.

xxvi Nekima Levy-Pounds, "Seeking Justice in the Age of Unrest," *The Crisis Magazine* 2015, https://www.thecrisismagazine.com/.

xxvii "Alt Right: A Primer About the New White Supremacy," *ADL*, accessed November 8, 2017, https://www.adl.org/education/resources/backgrounders/alt-right-a-primer-about-the-new-white-supremacy.

xxviii Ibid.

xxix Ibid.

xxx Ibid.

xxxi Ibid.

xxxii Russell Rickford, "Black Lives Matter," *New Labor Forum* 25. No. 1 (2016): 34–42, DOI: 10.1177/1095796015620171.

xxxiii The *Washington Post*, "Obama's Effort to Heal Racial Divisions and Uplift Black America."

xxxiv Trymaine Lee, "Donald Trump's Plan to Solve the Racial Divide," *MSNBC*, last modified March 22, 2016, http://www.msnbc.com/msnbc/donald-trumps-plan-solve-the-racial-divide.

xxxv Robert Miller, "Hurricane Katrina: Communications &

Infrastructure Impacts," National Defense University, January 2006, https://blackboard.angelo.edu/bbcswebdav/institution/LFA/CSS/Course%20Material/BOR4301/Readings/Hurricane%20Katrina%20Communications%20%26%20Infrastructure%20Impacts.pdf (accessed October 30, 2017).

xxxvi Monica Anderson and Paul Hitlin, "Social Media Conversations about Race," *Pew Research Center: Internet & Technology*, last modified August 15, 2016, http://www.pewinternet.org/2016/08/15/social-media-conversations-about-race/.

xxxvii Ibid.

xxxviii Ibid.

xxxix Katie Nodjimbadem, "The Long, Painful History of Police Brutality in the U.S.," *The Smithsonian.com*, last modified July 27, 2017, http://www.smithsonianmag.com/smithsonian-institution/long-painful-history-police-brutality-in-the-us-180964098/.

xl Nikita Carney, "All Lives Matter, but So Does Race: Black Lives Matter and the Evolving Role of Social Media," *Humanity & Society* 40, no. 2 (2016): 194, DOI: 10.1177/0160597616643868.

xli Ibid.

xlii Ibid.

xliii Greg Boyd, "Racism: Why Whites Have Trouble 'Getting It,'" *Evangelicals for Social Action*, last modified February 24, 2016, http://www.evangelicalsforsocialaction.org/racial-justice/racism-why-whites-have-trouble-getting-it/.

xliv Mark Schleifstein, "Study of Hurricane Katrina's Dead Show Most Were Old, Lived Near Levee Breaches," *The Times-Picayune*, October 8, 2009, http://www.nola.com/hurricane/index.ssf/2009/08/answers_ar

e_scarce_in_study_of.html.

xlv Ibid.

xlvi Ibid.

xlvii Stacey Mann, "Building Sustainable Cities in a Post-Katrina Nation: HR's Role in Mitigation and Planning," *Public Works Management & Policy* 17, no. 1 (2012):36 DOI: 10.1177/1087724X11429392.

xlviii Michael Eric Dyson, *Tears We Cannot Stop: A Sermon to White America* (New York: St. Martin's Press, 2017), 57-58.

xlix Missing source.

l Sabrina Toppa, "The Baltimore Riots Cost an Estimated $9 Million in Damages," *TIME*, last modified May 14, 2015, http://time.com/3858181/baltimore-riots-damages-businesses-homes-freddie-gray/.

li Nodjimbadem, "The Long, Painful History of Police Brutality in the U.S."

lii Wesley Lowery, "Aren't More White People Than Black People Killed by Police? Yes, but No," *The Washington Post*, last modified July 14, 2016, https://www.washingtonpost.com/news/post-nation/wp/2016/07/11/arent-more-white-people-than-black-people-killed-by-police-yes-but-no/?utm_term=.f65002a14199.

liii Nodjimbadem, "The Long, Painful History of Police Brutality in the U.S."

liv Ibid.

lv Manning Marable, "Racializing Obama: The Enigma of Post-Black Politics and Leadership," *Souls* 11 No. 1 (2009): 2 http://dx.doi.org.proxy.lib.duke.edu/10.1080/10999940902733202 (accessed October 30, 2017).

lvi Ian Haney López, *Dog Whistle Politics: How Coded Racial*

Appeals Have Reinvented Racism and Wrecked the Middle Class (New York: Oxford University Press, 2015), 10.

lvii Austin Channing Brown, "CTRL + ALT + DEL," *Austin Channing Brown*, July 8, 2013, accessed November 10, 2017, http://austinchanning.com/blog/2013/7/ctrl-alt-delete.

lviii Kendra Hadiya Barber, "What Happened to All the Protests?" *Journal of African American Studies* 15.2 (2011): 220.

lix Robert T. Carter, "Racism and Psychological and Emotional Injury: Recognizing and Assessing Race-Based Traumatic Stress," *The Counseling Psychologist* 35, no. 1 (2007): 79.

lx Barber, "What Happened to All the Protests?," 79.

lxi Lopez, *Dog Whistle Politics*, 103.

lxii Michelle Alexander, *The New Jim Crow: Mass Incarceration in the Age of Colorblindness* (New York: The New Press, 2012), 12.

lxiii Mark Hearn, "Color-Blind Racism, Color-Blind Theology, and Church Practices," *Religious Education* 104, no. 3 (2009): 273.

lxiv Hearn, "Color-Blind Racism," 277.

lxv Ibid.

lxvi Brown, "CTRL + ALT + DEL."

lxvii Joseph Barndt, *Dismantling Racism: The Continuing Challenge to White America* (Minneapolis: Augsburg, 1991), 57.

lxviii Rodney Clark, Norman B. Anderson, Vernessa R. Clark, David R. Williams, "Racism as a Stressor for African American: A Biopsychosocial Model," *American Psychologist* 54, no. 10 (October 1999): 805, accessed November 10, 2017.

lxix "Structural Racism Timeline," *Erase Racism*, accessed November 10, 2017, http://eraseracismny.org/component/content/article/17-teaching-tool/436-structural-racism-timeline.

lxx Frederick C. Harris and Robert C. Lieberman, "Racial Inequality After Racism: How Institutions Hold Back African

Americans," *Foreign Affairs*, accessed November 10, 2017, https://www.foreignaffairs.com/articles/united-states/2015-03-01/racial-inequality-after-racism.

lxxi Carol Anderson, *White Rage: The Unspoken Truth of Our Racial Divide* (New York: Bloomsbury 2017), 101.

lxxii Frederick C. Harris and Robert C. Lieberman, "Racial Inequality After Racism."

lxxiii Emerson and Smith use the term cultural "tool" in place of lens. I think lens is a better term given the direction of this book.

lxxiv Michael O. Emerson and Christian Smith, *Divided by Faith: Evangelical Religion and the Problem of Race in America* (New York: Oxford University Press, 2001), 76.

lxxv Ibid., 78.

lxxvi Ibid., 79.

lxxvii Carter, "Racism and Psychological and Emotional Injury," 30.

lxxviii Thema Bryant-Davis, "Healing Requires Recognition: The Case for Race-Based Traumatic Stress," *The Counseling Psychologist* 35, no. 1 (January 2007): 140, accessed November 10, 2017, DOI: 10.1177/0011000006295152. Thema Bryant Davis and Carlota Ocampo, "Racist Incident-Based Trauma," *The Counseling Psychologist* 33, no. 4 (July 2005) 479-500 DOI: 10.1177/0011000005276465.

lxxix Tim Wise, *Colorblind: The Rise of Post-Racial Politics and the Retreat from Racial Equity* (San Francisco: City Lights, 2010), 16.

lxxx Gary Bennett, Marcellus M. Merritt, and John J Sollers III, "Perceived Racism and Affective Responses to Ambiguous Interpersonal Interactions Among African American Men," *American Behavioral Scientist*, 47, no. 7 (March 2004): 964, accessed November 10, 2017, DOI: 10.1177/0002764203261070.

lxxxi Bryant-Davis and Ocampo, "Racist Incident-Based Trauma," 483.

lxxxii Bryant-Davis, "Healing Requires Recognition," 141.

lxxxiii Bryant-Davis, "Racist Incident Based Trauma," 483.

lxxxiv Christena Cleveland, "Psychological Homelessness in Your Church," *Christena Cleveland Blog*, October 16, 2012, accessed November 10, 2017, http://www.christenacleveland.com/blogarchive/2012/10/psychological-homelessness-in-your-church.

lxxxv Isaac Adams, "Why White Churches Are Hard for Black People," *9Marks*, last modified September 25, 2016, https://www.9marks.org/article/why-white-churches-are-hard-for-black-people/.

lxxxvi Katie Reilly, "Read President Obama's Speech From the Dallas Memorial Service," *TIME*, last modified July 12, 2016, http://time.com/4403543/president-obama-dallas-shooting-memorial-service-speech-transcript/.

lxxxvii Carroll Doherty, "Remembering Katrina: Wide Racial Divide Over Government's Response," *Factank*, last modified August 27, 2015, http://www.pewresearch.org/fact-tank/2015/08/27/remembering-katrina-wide-racial-divide-over-governments-response/.

lxxxviii David M. Abramson, Lynn M. Grattan, Brian Mayer, Craig E. Colten, Farah A. Arosemena, Ariane Bedimo-rung, and Maureen Lichtveld., "The Resilience Activation Framework: A Conceptual Model of How Access to Social Resources Promotes Adaptation and Rapid Recovery in Post-Disaster Settings," *The Journal of Behavioral Health Services & Research* 42, no. 1 (January 2015): 46, http://dx.doi.org/10.1007/s11414-014-9410-2.

lxxxix Boin, et al., *The Politics of Crisis Management*, 5.

xc Sinek, *Start with Why: How Great Leaders Inspire Everyone to Take Action* (New York: Portfolio/Penguin, 2011), 43.

xci L. Gregory Jones, *Christian Social Innovation: Renewing Wesleyan Witness* (Nashville: Abingdon Press, 2016), 42.

xcii Salter-McNeil, *Roadmap to Reconciliation*, 84.

xciii Rodin, *The Resilience Dividend*, 3.

xciv The National Academies, *Disaster Resilience: A National Imperative* (Washington, DC: National Academies Press, 2012).

xcv Rodin, *The Resilience Dividend*, 292.

xcvi Salter-McNeil, *Roadmap to Reconciliation*, 83.

xcvii Rodin, *The Resilience Dividend*, 199–200.

xcviii Dyson, *Tears We Cannot Stop*, 199.

xcix Briscoe, "Adaptation to Climate Change in the Houston Galveston Area," 27.

c Genesis 41:17–24 NLT.

ci Boin, Arjen, Paul T. Hart, Erik Stern, and Bengt Sundelius. *The Politics of Crisis Management: Public Leadership Under Pressure* (New York: Cambridge University Press, 2016), 15.

cii Ibid.

ciii Genesis 41: 25–32 NLT.

civ Genesis 41:33–36 NLT.

cv Genesis 41:37–43 NLT.

cvi Rodin, *Resilience Dividend*, 143.

cvii Abramson et al., "The Resilience Activation Framework," 42.

cviii Johnny Bernard Hill, *The First Black President: Barack Obama, Race, Politics, and the American Dream* (New York: Palgrave Macmillan, 2009), 56.

cix Sadowski and Sutter, "Mitigation Motivated by Past Experience," 304.

cx Dyson, *Tears We Cannot Stop*, 199.

cxi Rodin, *Resilience Dividend,* 124.

cxii "Cooperation," *Merriam-Webster*, accessed November 10, 2017, https://www.merriam-webster.com/dictionary/cooperation.

[cxiii] John Spencer, "The Difference Between Cooperation and Collaboration," *JS* (blog), June 22, 2016, http://www.spencerauthor.com/can-you-force-collaboration/.

[cxiv] Ibid.

[cxv] Ibid.

[cxvi] Paul W. Mattessich and Marta Murray-Close, *Collaboration: What Makes It Work, 2nd Edition: A Review of Research Literature on Factors Influencing Successful Collaboration* (Saint Paul, MN: Wilder Publishing Center, 2001), 61.

[cxvii] Ibid.

[cxviii] Rodin, *The Resilience Dividend*, 198.

[cxix] Arjen Boin, et al., *Designing Resilience*, 199.

[cxx] Ibid., 201.

[cxxi] Arjen Boin, et al., *The Politics of Crisis Management*, 74.

[cxxii] Ibid., 146.

[cxxiii] Nancy Rogers, Grande Lum, William Froehlich, "Planning in Advance of Civil Unrest," *Dispute Resolution Magazine* 22, no. 4, (Summer 2016): 1.

[cxxiv] Ibid.

[cxxv] "Community Relations Service," *The United States Department of Justice*, accessed November 10, 2017. https://www.justice.gov/crs/us-doj-community-relations-service.

[cxxvi] Rogers, Lum, and Froelich, "Planning in Advance of Civil Unrest," 2.

[cxxvii] Boin, Comfort, and Demchak, *Designing Resilience*, 201.

[cxxviii] Ibid.

[cxxix] John 17:23 NLT.

[cxxx] Masterson, Peacock, and Van Zandt, *Planning for Community*

Resilience, 22.

cxxxi Ibid., 64.

cxxxii Ibid.

cxxxiii Mark Kaplan and Mason Donovan, *The Inclusion Dividend Why Investing in Diversity & Inclusion Pays Off* (Brookline, MA: Bibliomotion, 2013), 212.

cxxxiv Ibid.

cxxxv Ibid.

cxxxvi Masterson, Peacock, Van Zandt, *Planning for Community Resilience*, 70.

cxxxvii Lovett H. Weems, *Church Leadership: Vision, Team, Culture, and Integrity* (Nashville: Abingdon Press, 2010), 36.

cxxxviii Ibid., 23.

cxxxix Ibid., 24.

cxl Ibid.

cxli Salter-McNeil, *Roadmap to Reconciliation*, 90.

cxlii Masterson, Peacock, Van Zandt, *Planning for Community Resilience*, 160–161.

cxliii Jim Wallis, Remembering King: Breaking the Silence, *Sojourners*, April 7, 2016, https://sojo.nct/articles/remembering-king-breaking-silence.

cxliv Ibid.

cxlv "What Is Linear Time vs. Nonlinear Time?," *Big Picture Questions.com*, accessed November 14, 2017. http://bigpicturequestions.com/what-is-linear-time-vs-nonlinear-time/.

cxlvi Kevin Clay, "The White Church Should Not Be Silent on the Killing of Black Men by Police," *The Root*, last modified October 6, 2014, https://www.theroot.com/the-white-church-should-not-be-silent-on-the-killing-of-1790877247.

cxlvii Bryan Massingale, "The Church's Appalling Silence On Racism," *U.S. Catholic Faith in Real Life*, January 23, 2017 http://www.uscatholic.org/articles/201701/churchs-appalling-silence-racism-30911.

cxlviii Watkins, "Do You Know What Your Pastor Will Say Tomorrow?"

cxlix Lim, "Tim Scott."

cl Gene M. Tucker, "The Role of the Prophets and the Role of the Church," *Quarterly Review* 5, no. 22 (1981): 159.

cli John Goldingay, *Old Testament Theology* (Downers Grove, Ill: InterVarsity Press, 2003).

clii 2 Samuel 12:7–10.

cliii Walter Brueggemann, "Prophetic Leadership: Engagement in Counter-Imagination," *Journal of Religious Leadership*, 10, no. 1 (Spring 2011): 10.

cliv Tucker, "The Role of the Prophets and the Role of the Church."

clv Emerson and Smith, "Divided by Faith," 164.

clvi Lischer, *The Preacher King,* 220.

clvii Ibid., 181.

clviii Lischer, Richard. *The Preacher King: Martin Luther King Jr. and the Word That Moved America*. New York: (Oxford University Press, 1997), 6.

clix Will Willimon, *Who Lynched Willie Earle?: Preaching to Confront Racism* (Nashville: Abingdon Press, 2017), 99.

clx Walter Brueggemann, *The Prophetic Imagination* (Minneapolis: Fortress Press, 1978), 13.

clxi Ibid., 72.

clxii Matthew 15:18–19 NLT.

clxiii Proverbs 18:13, 21 NLT.

clxiv 1 John 3:8.

clxv Brueggemann, *The Prophetic Imagination*, 13.

clxvi Austin Channing Brown "CTRL + ALT + DEL," *Austin Channing Brown*, July 8, 2013. accessed November 10, 2017, http://austinchanning.com/blog/2013/7/ctrl-alt-delete.

clxvii Austin Channing Brown "CTRL + ALT + DEL," *Austin Channing Brown*, July 8, 2013. accessed November 10, 2017, http://austinchanning.com/blog/2013/7/ctrl-alt-delete.

clxviii Dyson, *Tears We Cannot Stop*, 75, 76–77.

clxix Rodin, *The Resilience Dividend*, 247.

clxx Salter-McNeil, *Roadmap to Reconciliation*, 43.

clxxi Salter-McNeil, *Roadmap to Reconciliation*, 44.

clxxii Ibid., 45.

clxxiii Ibid.

clxxiv Ibid., 46–47.

clxxv Heifetz, *Leadership Without Easy Answers* (Cambridge: Harvard University Press, 1994), 22.

clxxvi Ibid.

clxxvii Salter-McNeil, *Roadmap to Reconciliation*, 46.

clxxviii Ibid, 52.

clxxix Heifetz, *Leadership Without Easy Answers*, 104.

clxxx Ibid.

clxxxi Ibid.

clxxxii Nannerl O. Keohane, *Thinking About Leadership* (Princeton, NJ: Princeton University Press, 2012), 19.

clxxxiii Rodin, *The Resilience Dividend*, 224.

clxxxiv Tierney, *The Social Roots of Risk,* 121.

clxxxv Ta-Nehisi Coates, *We Were Eight Years in Power: An*

American Tragedy (New York: One World Publishing, 2017), 225–226.

clxxxvi Ibid., 227.

clxxxvii Livia Gershon, "Did the 1965 Watts Riots Change Anything," *JStor Daily*, July 13, 2016, https://daily.jstor.org/did-the-1965-watts-riots-change-anything/.

clxxxviii James T. Patterson, "Moynihan and the Single-Parent Family: The 1965 Report and its Backlash," *Education Next* 15, no. 2 (Spring 2015): 6.

clxxxix Coates, *We Were Eight Years in Power*, 225.

Made in the USA
Columbia, SC
28 June 2020